Robert A. Heinlein

Twayne's United States Authors Series

Warren French, Editor

University College of Swansea, Wales

TUSAS 522

ROBERT A. HEINLEIN
Photo by William Corson, taken sometime between 1939 and 1941.
Reproduced courtesy of Virginia Heinlein.

Robert A. Heinlein

By Leon Stover

Illinois Institute of Technology

Twayne Publishers
A Division of G.K. Hall & Co. • *Boston*

Robert A. Heinlein

Leon Stover

Copyright 1987 by G.K. Hall & Co.
All rights reserved.
Published by Twayne Publishers
A Division of G.K. Hall & Co.
70 Lincoln Street
Boston, Massachusetts 02111

Copyediting supervised by Lewis DeSimone
Book production by John Amburg
Book design by Barbara Anderson

Typeset in 11 pt. Garamond
by Williams Press, Inc., Albany, New York

Library of Congress Cataloging in Publication Data

Stover, Leon E.
  Robert A. Heinlein.
  (Twayne's United States authors series ; TUSAS 522)
  Bibliography: p.
  Includes index.
  1. Heinlein, Robert A. (Robert Anson), 1907–
Criticism and interpretation. 2. Science Fiction,
American—History and criticism. I. Title. II. Series.
PS3515.E288Z88 1987   813'.54   87-14876
ISBN 0-8057-7509-9 (alk. paper)

j

for
Takeko

Contents

About the Author

Leon Stover is professor of Anthropology at the Illinois Institute of Technology, where he teaches a course on Robert A. Heinlein, two on H. G. Wells, and another on modern science fiction. For the latter survey course he published two readers, and soon after was commissioned by the Sorbonne to write *La Science Fiction Américaine* (1972), a textbook for its program in American studies.

Before coming to IIT in 1965, he was for two years a visiting professor at Tokyo University where, as the first non-Japanese to teach in its graduate school, he was invited to develop his new theory of China. His lectures there are published as a trade book, *The Cultural Ecology of Chinese Civilization* (1974), and, with the aid of his wife, as a textbook, *China: An Anthropological Perspective* (1976). Thereafter he turned to European prehistory with *Stonehenge and the Origins of Western Culture* (1979). But he first played with his new political interpretation of that monument in a novel written with Harry Harrison, a fellow member of Science Fiction Writers of America, now enlarged as *Stonehenge: Where Atlantis Died* (1983).

As a member of the H. G. Wells Society, he wrote his most recent book, *The Prophetic Soul: A Reading of H. G. Wells's "Things to Come"* (1987), and on the fiftieth anniversary of the movie he lectured at the National Film Theatre, London, by invitation of the British Film Institute. Earlier he did a work of Wellsian literary criticism in the form of a dialogue novel, *The Shaving of Karl Marx* (1982). In 1986 he served as Humanities Consultant to the Champaign Public Library and the University of Illinois Library, Urbana, to help mount a Traveling H. G. Wells Exhibition.

Leon Stover holds a Ph.D. in anthropology and China studies from Columbia University. In 1980 he was awarded an honorary Doctor of Letters (Litt.D.) from his undergraduate alma mater, Western Maryland College, where he majored in English. Before that he graduated from George School in Bucks County, Pennsylvania, his home state (born 1929). When Pennsylvania still was frontier country, it was pioneered by both the Heinleins and the Stovers after their first ancestors arrived there from Bavaria almost the same year in the mid-1700s. Both family lines mothered a U.S. president.

Preface

Walt Whitman in his essay, "Democratic Vistas" (1871), urged the American eagle to fly on its own literary wings. No more borrowings from the decadent medieval culture of European feudalism! He called upon United States authors to celebrate America's different "moral identity" in a future-regarding "literature of science . . . that is bold, modern and all-surrounding and kosmical, as she herself is." In his Preface to the 1865 edition of *Leaves of Grass* he said it before: let us have imaginative writers befitting this "nation of nations" and her cosmic destiny.

Who more than Robert A. Heinlein, "the dean of American science fiction writers," has answered that call? Heretofore, academic critics have treated Heinlein as a subject fit only for their new fringe field of science-fiction studies, locating him in some deracinated outland beyond the pale of classical American letters. This work is the first to treat him as a significant American author and not merely as a genre writer.

After all, what is now called science fiction (SF by its fans) used to be published in the general magazines by the likes of Nathaniel Hawthorne, Edgar Allan Poe, Herman Melville, Ambrose Bierce, Fitz-James O'Brien, and Mark Twain.[1] But their science-fiction stories never were regarded in their own time as anything other than as a part of general fiction. Indeed, America's first professional novelist, Charles Brockden Brown, wrote largely in this genre.

By the twentieth century, however, American fiction came to be dominated by a mundane concern for historical veracity. If it wasn't realistic or sublunary, if it dealt with the strange and the wonderful—in short, if it were romantic—it wasn't literature with a capital L. Never mind that so-called naturalistic writers like Theodore Dreiser, in their wonderful attention to the imponderabilia of everyday life, actually raised realism to transcendental heights. Indeed, according to Roger Asselineau, Europe's foremost critic of American literature, this is the very hallmark of mainstream American fiction, unlike anything in European or English letters.[2] For all that, the outrightly romantic went underground, surviving only in the lowbrow magazines of popular culture with their mainly juvenile readers.

Here science fiction got its name as a separate publisher's category in 1926, during that gaudy era of the pulp magazine trade that lasted in full flush from the turn of the century until the early 1940s, just before the advent of World War II. It was here, in 1939, that Heinlein began his astonishing literary career.

Immediately after the war, he was the first to bring science fiction out of its pulpish ghetto into the wider market it reaches today. By 1961, he was the first of his fellow genre writers to make the best-seller list of the *New York Times,* and has done so again and again.

There is good reason for this. Heinlein brought something classy to magazine science fiction it never had before, when it circulated only among teenaged fans. That extra something is a natural gift for storytelling, informed by adult experience (he started late), and a knowing regard for the native literary heritage.

Heinlein so improved the genre with the quality of his polished example, that he must be regarded as rather more the shaper of modern science fiction than as its most famous product. Yet despite his influence (mainly in upgrading craft), he remains distinctive. He alone is a naturalist of the romantic. His work thus converges upon the classical mainstream from the other side of realism, altogether in keeping with that "transcendental constant" Professor Asselineau finds in American literature.

But it was his discerning fans, not the literati, who from the start raised Heinlein to eminence within the field itself. It was they, early on at one of their conventions (or "cons" in fannish language), who named him "the dean of American science-fiction writers," and who keep on voting him their "best all-time author."

Myself a sometime con-goer and voter, and a Heinlein fan for well over forty years (the last twenty or more given to teaching science fiction), it will come as no surprise that I write as both fan and critic, following a precedent set by Henry James, who came very close to recommending the same combined approach. Literary criticism, said James, is a "supremely beneficent" thing. The critic is to serve as the "real helper of the artist, a torch-bearing outrider, the interpreter, the brother," who is "keyed up" to the beauty and craft of the author he chooses to treat out of his "curiosity and sympathy."[3]

James did not mean, however, that the critic need be incandescent about everything done by the subject of his favoring light. When looking back on Mark Twain, "the father of our national literature" as H. L. Mencken said, we find that very little of his voluminous work is today considered worth rereading. But how great that little! What works of

Heinlein are worth more critical attention than others? What little, or more, of Heinlein's will the future hold dear?

To be sure, any literary work must be active in relation to a buyer's market, else it would not see print. So it has been for every classic of the language that has outlasted its original salesworthiness. But what makes the difference between the transiently popular and the lasting? What makes for the selecting out from the complete works of Mark Twain those now considered classics? No less than Heinlein, he wrote not for critical patronage but for the trade.

Perhaps this is consistent with the fact that Heinlein himself strongly resists being interpreted by any critical mode whatsoever, as I learned during my visit with him (at the age of nearly seventy-seven) in June 1984. No meaning to any of it, he says. "Entertainment" is all, paid for in cash and sold on the market like any other commercial product.

These are mysteries I have not the wisdom to penetrate. And so I fall back with James in the belief that fanship—"curiosity and sympathy"—will suffice for criticism. All the same, I hope my partisan treatment will invite readers unfamiliar with Heinlein to discover him and make their own judgments. There is, after all, plenty to choose from: more than forty-five book titles (novels and short story collections) done over nearly fifty years, all still in print.

As for the millions of Heinlein fans worldwide, there will be no pleasing them whatever line of emphasis is taken. For them, however, I append the following lines, done in a serious parody of Walt Whitman. They will recognize "Up Ship!" as the title of a poem by the blind bard of the spaceways in "The Green Hills of Earth," for which the story provides no text. They will also note that I have worked in two of Heinlein's most famous neologisms, "free fall" and "astrogation," not overlooking "n-dimensional space," his original locution for the hyperspace of science-fiction convention.

Up Ship!

Starship captains say it in the space navy,
   in the merchant marine of space,
   and in the passenger service.
It is the only intelligible language of space,
   used by those undocking and leaving and casting off
   from planetary stations.

ROBERT A. HEINLEIN

Up Ship!
It is the captain's language of free fall
   and astrogation,
Ever going somewhere in the nowhere of
   n-dimensional space.
Where he goes and from where, that is known.
Why he goes and what cosmic destiny he reaches,
   that is not known.

Illinois Institute of Technology

Leon Stover

Acknowledgments

My first debt of gratitude goes to Robert and Virginia Heinlein, whom my wife and I were privileged to visit in their home on 9 June 1984. For their hospitality, fine talk, tour of their ten-thousand-volume library, and some follow-up correspondence—all that amounts to more gracious help than I dared to expect.

I hope their permission to let me quote from the works of Robert A. Heinlein at my discretion has not been abused. They were generous enough also to supply the frontispiece and the appendix.

What I learned from letters answering a few belated questions, it would be overly pedantic to footnote. Besides, these often repeat similar accounts to be found in two recent press interviews. The first is, "Robert A. Heinlein: A Conservative View of the Future" by Patrick Cox in the *Wall Street Journal* for 10 December 1985 (p. 30f.). The other is, "The Man Who Writes through Time" by Eric Hoffman, in the *San Francisco Examiner* for 9 February 1986, in its magazine section *Image* (pp. 18–29, 40–42).

Were it not for my field editor, Warren French, however, this book would not exist. I am indebted to him (just retired from Indiana University) for upholding my proposal to find Heinlein a worthy subject for Twayne's United States Authors Series, and for the vast intelligence of his unstinting editorial help.

I am honored to thank Roger Asselineau, lately retired from the University of Paris IV, for corresponding with me on the question of what it is that gives American literature its native identity.

Closer than any to this project is my wife, Takeko Kawai Stover, who journeyed with it first and last, from Heinlein visit to final draft.

Randy Tomaszewski of the IIT Library did me the most unusual services with steadfast purpose whenever called upon.

Finally, it is only proper that I thank the many students enrolled in my Heinlein course over the years, from whom I have learned much about his appeal to readers of their age everywhere.

Chronology

1958, *Have Space Suit—will Travel,* may very well turn out to be one of his masterworks.

1948   Marries Lt. Virginia Gerstenfeld, a former WAVE officer, chemist, and aeronautical test engineer he met at Mustin Field.

1950   Moves to Denver, Colorado, to recuperate from TB in the Fitzsimmons hospital.

1956   Receives Hugo Award for *Double Star,* and again in 1960 for *Starship Troopers* (a juvenile not in the Scribner's series). This is a fans' award given in honor of Hugo Gernsback, who named science fiction when in 1926 he published the first of the pulps in this genre. Hugos have been awarded annually since 1955.

1962   Hugo Award for *Stranger in a Strange Land,* the first science-fiction novel to make the *New York Times* bestseller list.

1966   Moves back to California where he and his wife now reside in Santa Cruz County in house of his own design.

1967   Another Hugo Award for *The Moon is a Harsh Mistress.*

1970 & 1973   Publishes two long novels, *I Will Fear No Evil* and *Time Enough for Love.* The latter (a best-seller) resumes the epic of Lazarus Long, begun in a prewar novel, *Methuselah's Children,* in the Future History series.

1973   Delivers James Forrestal Memorial Lecture, "Channel Markers," at his Annapolis alma mater (5 April).

1975   Given the first Grand Masters Award by Science Fiction Writers of America, a professional society founded in 1965.

1978   Recovers from a carotid bypass operation, following a near stroke or transient ischemic attack. Reprints as a gift book "The Notebooks of Lazarus Long" from *Time Enough for Love.*

1979   Testifies before a joint session of the House Select Committee on Aging, and before the House Committee on Science and Technology, re Applications of Space Technology for the Elderly and Handicapped (19 July).

1980   Returns to new work with *The Number of the Beast* (another best-seller), full of anagrams and in-jokes. See Appendix for the anagrams.

1984   At age seventy-seven, makes the *New York Times* best-seller list again with *Job: A Comedy of Justice*.

1985   Another best-seller, *The Cat Who Walks through Walls*. Lazarus Long appears again, as he does in *Number of the Beast*.

1987   *To Sail beyond the Sunset,* the autobiography of Lazarus Long's mother, published on 7 July, Heinlein's eightieth birthday.

Chapter One

The Admiral and Mark Twain

It is 9 June 1984. As a historian of World War II, picking over the last scraps of oral testimony, I interview a five-star admiral named Robert A. Heinlein, living in retirement among the redwoods he loves in Santa Cruz County, California. He was commander of the U. S. Third Fleet in the South Pacific Area, and had stood with General Douglas MacArthur and Rear Admiral Chester Nimitz on the deck of the battleship *Missouri* (named after his home state) in Tokyo Bay, to preside over the surrender ceremonies marking the defeat of the Japanese Empire. I found him busy writing technical briefs for his private consulting firm, under a U. S. Government contract to advise on the national Space Defense Initiative, and so I left him. . . .

But wait. Wasn't it a carrier admiral named William "Bull" Halsey who commanded the Third Fleet? Yes; but not in the far more likely world of might-have-been. Elsewhere and elsewhen in this mighty pluriverse of ours that science-fiction writers are fond of exploring, with its parallel worlds of alternative probability, Admiral Heinlein is indeed writing his engineering reports out there in California at this very moment. Improbable? No more so than what actually happened in this particular universe. So let's replay that opening scene in light of the really weird and wonderful here and now.

It is 9 June 1984. I pay a visit to retired Navy Lieutenant Robert A. Heinlein, dwelling in a house of his own design set among the redwoods he loves in Santa Cruz County. A month short of seventy-seven, he still is active in his alternative career. A graduate of the U. S. Naval Academy at Annapolis, he was invited by his alma mater in 1973 to deliver the James V. Forrestal Memorial Lecture. Addressing the brigade of midshipmen with all the commanding presence and tough-minded moral authority of a grizzled fleet admiral, and in the name of a former Secretary of Defense, he spoke of courage, duty, honor, patriotism. Yet he carried this off altogether by virtue of his

1

nonmilitary repute—won in the bulked-pulp pages of *Astounding Science Fiction*.[1]

One of the midshipmen seated in that audience to hear "Channel Markers," as Heinlein titled his address, later was posted to the Naval ROTC program at the Illinois Institute of Technology. Ten years after the event, the lecture remained vivid in his memory, and he recalled the guidance it gave him in steering his life between the absolutes of right and wrong, good and bad, true and false, real and unreal, just and unjust.

It was for him a familiar lesson, however, enforced by the speaker's presence, for the midshipman had been a Heinlein reader in high school before he joined the Academy. He mentioned with special favor the juvenile series Heinlein wrote between 1947 and 1959. Indeed, it was he and his fellow fans who had invited Heinlein to Annapolis. They all knew who he was. So that Heinlein had no need to say a word about himself when he appeared. The moral values these midshipmen found of merit in his life work, he merely repeated without self-reference. Their previous reading had well disposed them to receive his commanding presence and to accept on faith, in this relativistic world of soft ethics, his authority to lay out life's true channel markers. No less would they have followed him in battle, this imposing man gifted with the natural qualities of leadership.

But Heinlein was not fated to lead men in uniform, although his career in the navy began with every sign of leading on to the highest rank. Graduating from Annapolis twentieth out of 243 in the class of 1929, with the gold stripe of ensign, he thereafter officered the gunnery on various destroyers and then on the battleship USS *Utah,* before he was promoted to serve on the Navy's first modern aircraft carrier, the USS *Lexington*. During one of its training exercises, before it sailed off to glory in the Pacific war, he was assigned as radio compass officer, responsible for all planes in the air and for bringing them back safely. In untried operations war games can be as dangerous as the real thing; and in this one a crisis arose whose make-or-break judgment fell to Heinlein alone. How he decided it is told in the modestly disguised fiction, "Searchlight." Only much later did he reveal the story's autobiographical details, in a collection of fact and fiction, *Expanded Universe*.[2]

In 1934, however, his intended career as a professional military man of proven worth was cut short by a medical discharge. Tuberculosis.

All the same, to his friends and knowing fans, both in and out of the navy, he is none other than "The Admiral."

Like the consumptive H. G. Wells, diverted from a teaching career after study at London's Normal School of Science, Heinlein turned to writing almost at random following a period of collapse and near dying. But there is another connection. During my visit with Heinlein and a tour of his huge library, he was pleased to show me his autographed reprint copy of *When the Sleeper Wakes,* one of the Scientific Romances of H. G. Wells first published in 1898. Wells had signed it for him when on a trip to California in 1935, just four years before Heinlein began writing. Handing it to me in silent reverence, eyes agleam, he knew what I would make of it without explanation. For writers and fans alike, Wells is "the father of modern science fiction," and its American deanship they bestowed upon Heinlein as a form of Wellsian sonhood.

A parallel with the TB-ridden Robert Louis Stevenson also comes to mind. Moreover, both he and Heinlein have early demonstrated their talent in juvenile fiction. What Henry James judged to be the outstanding quality of Stevenson's youthful work applies to Heinlein: "What makes him so [rare] is the singular maturity of the expression that he has given to young sentiments: he judges them, measures them, sees them from the outside, as well as entertains them. He describes credulity with all the resources of experience, and represents a crude stage with infinite ripeness. In a word, he is an artist accomplished even to sophistication, whose constant theme is the unsophisticated. Sometimes . . . the execution is so serious that the idea (the idea of a boy's romantic adventures) becomes a matter of universal relations."[3]

Closer to home is the familiar case of Samuel Langhorne Clemens, a fellow Missourian, who became Mark Twain after his career as a riverboat pilot on the Mississippi was cut off by the Civil War. But quite apart from their accidental drift into writing, the two are linked in literary kinship far closer than Heinlein's to Wells or to any other science fiction writer. Indeed, Twain is his favorite American author, whose complete works (even the obscurest) he keeps in his library. These influenced him more than did the science-fiction magazines he read as a youth.

For one thing, Heinlein writes in that conversational tone of voice pioneered by Twain the frontier raconteur and teller of tall tales. His easygoing narrative rhythms contrast with the formal periods of high-toned eloquence associated with really serious and deep-thinking writers.

Yet it serves a purpose no less weighty. As Twain said to an interviewer in 1900, "I disseminate my true views by means of a series of apparently humorous and mendacious stories."[4] So too with Heinlein. He tells his truth disguised as tall tales and with the same conversational ease, carried along by a steady undercurrent of good-natured humor.

(For what else are science-fiction stories, if not the tall tales of the backwoodsman, his frontier lore updated with modern shop talk? A perfectly smooth example is " '—And He Built a Crooked House—,' " which draws upon the mathematical chatter of fourth-dimensional geometry as given out by the American architect Claude Bragdon, in his little classic of 1913, *A Primer of Higher Space*. The fabulous twist to the Heinlein story occurs when there is an earthquake that causes the tesseract house of the story's title—an unfolded hypercube built in three dimensions—to shake down and fold up into a 4-D shape as would be the case with a true hypercube, all of its exterior surfaces joined one with another. If the architect then looks out the window of one room to see himself from the backside looking out that same window, his line of vision but follows that predicated by serious geometers in speculating how the fourth dimension, in abstract theory, might actually be experienced.)

In this, both writers share in the Puritan heritage of plain speaking and the avoidance of ornamental niceties. At the same time, such a style is not easy to cultivate because it imitates the informal cadences of natural speech. It imitates, but does not copy, as is evident from listening to any sample of everyday talk played back on a tape recorder. Every author who uses this technique (Ernest Hemingway is another masterly example) produces a unique result. Each imprints his personal signature on the natural model. Spontaneous and self-expressive as the speaking tone of voice may sound in the reader's inner ear, it is never a product of the writer's lack of discipline.

Heinlein himself defines the writer as a "word-carpenter." This is exactly right. It is the very meaning the Greeks gave to the eponym of their greatest poet. "Homer" simply means "word-joiner," as joinery is understood by any carpenter. No less, then, is Heinlein's conversational style a product of craft and studied art. Still, it is as far removed from stylistic artiness as it is possible to get.

This contrast, at its wildest extremes, is evident in the difference between Heinlein and (a favored author for all that) E. A. Poe. Here is the opening sentence from Poe's "Fall of the House of Usher": "During the whole of a dull, dark, and soundless day in the autumn of the year, when the clouds hung oppressively low in the heavens, I had been passing alone, on horseback, through a singularly dreary tract of country, and at length found myself, as the shades of the evening drew on, within view of the melancholy House of Usher." Note the deadly serious drumming of the *d*'s (alliteration) and the doom-laden wailing of the *o*'s (assonance). The nightmarish aspect of the House of Usher is played up by such fancy rhetoric.

Compare it with the way Heinlein plays down the opening lines of *The Door into Summer*.

One winter shortly before the Six Weeks War my tomcat, Petronius the Arbiter, and I lived in an old farmhouse in Connecticut. I doubt if it is there any longer, as it was near the edge of the blast area of the Manhattan near-miss, and those old frame buildings burn like tissue paper. Even if it is still standing it would not be a desirable rental because of the fallout, but we liked it then, Pete and I.

Here, with no nightmare effects, the reader is eased into a horrible future that is a commonplace for the narrator. Describing it in the casual phrases of everyday speech, he makes it all the more real, the awful setting seemingly domesticated and made ready for the reader to move in feeling at home with the situation from the start.[5]

Poe is the most important romancer in the early history of American science fiction before it got its name in the later genre magazines. Although he figures in the awareness of all native writers in this field, their response to his work divides on the basis of the very stylistic lines exemplified above. His most stylish heir is Ray Bradbury, who has a following second only to Heinlein's, but few of these fans overlap. (Standing in between is Isaac Asimov, an equally big name and a notable award winner as well, whose prose is neither literary nor informal but merely artless—as he is the first to admit.) The two are in fact at odds with each other on rhetorical grounds alone. Bradbury's alliterative and assonant fireworks, as in his high-voltage phrase about a chicken's "cold cut guts," are not to science-fiction fans' universal liking, but surely please official tastemakers.

No such passages are found in Heinlein. For him, the task of style is not to call attention to itself, nor to render the strange and wonderful all the more exotic, but to make such things as homely as a well-worn bedroom slipper. Bradbury has a large following, but he has yet to win a Hugo Award from the fans or a Nebula Award from the writers, much less one of their Grand Master Awards. For the literati, however, he is Mr. Science Fiction, in spite of the deanship conferred on Heinlein by these others, if only because Bradbury's high-toned rodomontade seems to give a serious gloss to what is little more than *faux naïveté,* a false innocence that is not exactly calculated to help mature his adolescent readers. There is a popular market for his manner to be sure, but it is not Heinlein's. It may appeal to the academics and the intellectuals and the critics, by way of patronizing the unripe young. But the work of Heinlein echoes a different note, that voiced by Twain when he said, "I have never tried in one single instance to help cultivate the cultivated classes. . . . And I never had any ambition in that direction, but always hunted for bigger game—the masses."[6]

Heinlein hunts the same game, and has done so with like success and with a similar purpose, which so much galls his cultivated academic critics. Twain might have been Heinlein speaking of his own tall tales, with all their low-keyed wit, when Twain said, "Humor must not professedly teach and it must not professedly preach, but it must do both if it would live forever."[7] By "forever" he meant about thirty years. But he did much better than that, and so will Heinlein with his best.

After James Fenimore Cooper, Twain was the first major American author to whom readers turned with no thought of moral uplift or self-improvement. Fully half the books of Colonial America were collected church sermons, the rest mainly how-to manuals for this or that practical thing, the one publisher's category of the native Puritan heritage that remains undiminished in popularity to this day.

Certainly the Great Humorist (the Great Moralist to those not amused) did nothing to hurt sales, promoted door-to-door by subscription agents, by suggesting anything other than his advertised purpose. Twain's facetious "Notice" facing the opening page of *Huckleberry Finn,* his one true classic, warns that, "Persons attempting to find a motive in this narrative will be prosecuted; persons attempting to find a moral will be banished."

Heinlein markets himself the same way. In the facetious words of his Foreword to *Expanded Universe,* he disavows anything but the emptiest of huckstering. "Each copy is guaranteed—or double your money back—to be printed on genuine paper of enough pages to hold the covers apart" (*EU,* 3). One of his viewpoint characters, a businessman artist not unlike himself, says that all he cares for is "praise from the customer, given in cash."[8]

But, of course, Heinlein is no less didactic than Twain, and is read for both his wit and his wisdom. He gets fan mail from all over the world, whose mostly youthful writers (handwriting on lined paper is the usual form) almost invariably address him as their "spiritual father." I was privileged to hear some of these letters read aloud by his wife, yet Heinlein insisted (using Graham Greene's word) that he wrote nothing but "entertainments." Even granted that, I said, quoting Aristotle, any fiction has its *muthos* and its *praxis* (its manifest story line and its invisible ideas hidden within this other), no literary text says all that it signifies. He cut me off, however, suggesting that I had missed the obvious! After all, he said, he'd have nothing to write about if he hadn't "some consistent world view in the back of my mind."

Both Twain and Heinlein also continued to identify themselves with broken careers, long after they found their authentic calling. At Quarry Farm in Elmira, New York, Mark Twain did his pencil work in a writing studio built to the likeness of a Mississippi riverboat's pilothouse. Hanging on the wall in front of Heinlein's word processor is a framed "Certificate of Satisfactory Service," signed by James V. Forrestal (who was, incidentally, not only Secretary of Defense but the first federal official to be for space travel).

As it happens, this document is not The Admiral's but his wife's. She received it when going off duty with the navy at the end of World War II, during which time Heinlein met her at Mustin Field. Stuck into the frame is a small photo of her in uniform taken at that time, a reminder that, like Twain, Heinlein is a uxorious homebody. "Samuel Clemens put it: 'Where she was, there was Eden.' "9

But the fleet still remains his alternative home. "I was sworn in first in 1925 and have not been off the hook since that time" (*EU* 397f.). Rightly proud of the military profession he started out to serve, he has kept himself on the rolls of the U. S. Naval Academy Alumni Association, the Naval Institute, and the Retired Officers Association. He also holds advisory status in the Navy League, the Air Force Association, the Air Power Council, and the Association of the Army of the United States.

This helps explain why Heinlein is the self-confident man, like Twain, still at home in his pilothouse. During their early careers, both men learned that with command and authority comes responsibility (the point driven home in Heinlein's prewar story, "The Roads Must Roll," which is pertinent as ever in light of the air controllers' strike of 1981, as is "Blowups Happen" in light of the Chernobyl disaster of 1986). Or more likely, they were self-selected for the demands of duty by temperament and character. At all events, Heinlein likes and enjoys himself as only a person once charged with the lives of others self-confidently can. By contrast, the neurotic writers of the modernist movement seem to relish morbid self-interest, as if the agonies of the creative act and their vulgar confession were the only possible trademarks of sincerity. Not for him "The Artist as Exemplary Sufferer," to cite the title of one of Susan Sontag's essays in *Against Interpretation* (1966).

Even Twain's frontier experience has its match in Heinlein's upbringing. The American past and its frontier ethos is more than a bookish memory for him; and this explains why Heinlein is able to project its pioneering future, on those new frontiers of outer space opened up by D. D. Harriman in "The Man Who Sold the Moon," with such a familiar sense of lived-in vividness. He is able to recall anecdotes passed down in the Heinlein Family Association from his "triple great grandfather" who settled in Ohio, a place then on the verge of the wild unknown, following the landing of his first American ancestor from Bavaria, in Philadelphia on 31 October 1754. This was Matheis Heinlein who, with his wife, two daughters, and son George, settled on a tract of partly farmed land in Durham township, Bucks County, Pennsylvania. Son George served as captain of the Durham township militia and fought throughout the entire period of the Revolutionary War, to be buried with honors on the family plantation at his death at sixty-three in 1805. Through him all the Heinleins are descended. Robert's triple great-grandfather of anecdotal memory was one of four Heinleins from among George's grandsons and great-grandsons to move with their entire families to Ohio in about 1860. Thereafter, Heinleins pushed steadily westward, others keeping behind in a natural process of selection that sorts out the pioneers from the sedents.

A similar westward progression is evident on Robert Heinlein's maternal side. His mother's father, Dr. Alva E. Lyle (d. 1914), like his paternal grandfather, was one of Missouri's earliest settlers. He served rural Butler and vicinity as a country doctor, living long enough into Robert's boyhood to have his young grandson as a seat companion for several summers on his horse-and-buggy rounds. A strong influence, Heinlein is happy to remember, the doctor taught the boy to play chess at age four even before he learned to read. No doubt the talk he passed of evenings over the chessboard is reflected in the crusty aphorisms of the elderly Lazarus Long, himself a pioneer, leading the Howard families in their great diaspora "out into the Endless Deeps".[10] Like grandfather Lyle, he possesses just those traits that make for survival in the pioneering of any frontier: physical vigor and courage, shrewd self-reliance, and a puritanical moral toughness grounded in what both Heinlein and Twain like to call "horse sense"—at bottom a mistrust of theoretical abstractions and a practical regard for empirical reality.

The same frontier code animates the wild-west, laissez-faire economics of D. D. Harriman, often to the point of cunning duplicity. He is named (no doubt) after the nineteenth-century financier and railroad magnate, Edward Henry Harriman, one of the five robber barons execrated by Archibald MacLeish in "Empire Builders" (1933), a poem about "The Making [ironically the corruption] of America in Five Panels." The Museum Attendant begins:

> This is Mister Harriman making America:
> Mister-Harriman-is-buying-the-Union-pacific-at-Seventy:
> The Santa Fe is shining on his hair.

Approaching the same age, the graying D. D. Harriman gets moonlight shining on his hair. But Heinlein holds no MacLeish-like brief against him. Far from it. One of Harriman's associates pays him the tribute of calling him "the last of the Robber Barons." But another does better, saying, "Not the last. The last of them opened up the American West. He's the first of the *new* Robber Barons—and you and I won't see the end of it. Do you ever read Carlyle?"[11] This is Heinlein's tribute as well, extended to a Carlyle-like hero given by destiny to change the course of history at one of its needful turning points. By founding Luna City, freeport to the outer planets and beyond, he delivers free enterprise from statist captivity into the boundless reaches of unclosable frontiers, ensuring human progress once and for all, forever.

Heinlein always writes as The Admiral, never substituting emotive self-expression for the discipline of his craft. He is altogether normal and decent, "one sane man" as described by Damon Knight, a leading science-fiction writer turned critic.[12] For Heinlein himself, sanity is a matter of homely "horse sense," as codified in the "Notebooks of Lazarus Long" (hereafter *LL*), contained within *Time Enough for Love*. These notebooks are filled with practical witticisms not unlike those of "Pudd'nhead Wilson's Calendar" in Twain's novel, *Pudd'nhead Wilson*, whose hero's head is made of pudding only in the view of his fellow townsmen. They pride themselves on their "common sense," which is nothing of the sort; their use of the phrase is a pleasing illusion, serving only to hide from sight the hard truths of everyday reality that is

Wilson's gift alone to discern. The same with the notebook-writing Lazarus Long, who says, "that phrase is self-contradictory. 'Sense' is never 'common' " (*LL*, 260). Another Heinlein hero speaks of "the stalwart common sense of ignorance and prejudice."[13] For both Twain and Heinlein, "horse sense" names the real thing, taken as a normative ideal.

In addition, both authors are notable above all for their so-called juvenile fiction. With Twain, it is *The Adventures of Huckleberry Finn* and *The Adventures of Tom Sawyer*, what he called his "boy's and girl's books." Heinlein casts up the same phrase when he talks about the dozen or so works of a like sort he himself did. At least one of these, *Have Space Suit—Will Travel*, or maybe *Starman Jones*, is in time likely to be rated as highly as *Huckleberry Finn*, or as R. L. Stevenson's *Treasure Island*.

The first generation of boys and girls to read Twain's juveniles grew up to reread them as adults and to rediscover them as epics of "universal relations" (to recall James's phrase). Every new generation since then has done the same, which is how classics are born in a democracy. They are made by readers, not by the gurus of high culture. That spirit was recognized by William Dean Howells, the lone man of letters to boost Twain in his own time on the grounds that American literature can fulfill the democratic experience only if it holds itself to everyday "sense and truth"—a quality better tested by its mass of readers than by learned critics. With that confident insight, he hailed Twain as the "Lincoln of our literature."[14] And it was Hemingway who remarked in *Green Hills of Africa* that all truly American fiction comes out of *Huckleberry Finn*.

Those who read and reread Heinlein are now making classics of his boy's books, modeled as they are in their own original way after his worthy exemplar. He, too, impersonates teenage narrators without writing down, achieving the same success that Mark Twain did with the voice of Huck Finn, that boy-man who is none other than the American "Ulysses of the many wiles" (Homer's tag line), a wandering hero up against forces greater than himself who yet triumphs over them. This is the real stuff of literature, making for return readers, again and again, because it presents the genuine epic of life. Heinlein understands what he is doing with perfect clarity. As he says in "Ray Guns and Rocket Ships," an article for school librarians, "a book so juvenile that it will insult the intelligence of adults is quite likely to insult the intelligence of the kids. Science Fiction for children should also interest adult readers." To be specific, he goes on, such values "as honor, loyalty, fortitude, self-sacrifice, bravery, honesty, and integrity will be as important in the far reaches of the Galaxy as they are in Iowa or Korea."[15]

Heinlein's originality lies in suiting his model of moral instruction to youngsters with a taste for science fiction—a genre little noted for its humor, much less for winning its way onto lists of juvenile reading favored by American school librarians. As with Twain, his humor arises not so much from the action, but rather from the roguish tone of the first-person narration itself.

For example, take Poddy, the adolescent girl-woman who narrates *Podkayne of Mars* (not part of the Scribner's juvenile series). "That's me: Poddy Fries, free citizen of Mars, female. Future pilot and someday commander of deep-space exploration parties. Watch for me in the news."[16] Before getting caught up in her adventures, she talks of her wish to visit Earth. "Not live, of course—just to see it. As everybody knows, Terra is a wonderful place to visit but not to live. Not truly suited to human habitation." Indeed, she disbelieves the story that humans, now living throughout the solar system, had their origin on that planet, unfit for living as it presently is. She wonders "how in the world eight billion people manage to live almost sitting in each other's laps." As a Martian adapted to a semi-arid planet, however, she'd like to see Earth's exotic oceans—but "from a safe distance," she adds. "Oceans are not only fantastically unlikely but to me the very thought of them is terrifying. All that unimaginable amount of water, unconfined. And so deep that if you fell into it, it would be over your head. Incredible!" (*PM*, 7).

The mischief done here is all in the rhetoric, a prank played on the reader's complacency with a limited worldview. A commonplace feature of our world is made to look unfamiliar, by way of a distancing technique called "making strange" by Ezra Pound, or "defamiliarization" in the technical vocabulary of literary criticism. It is a humorous form of irony, whose technique the reader is expected to see through, and therefore get the joke.[17]

With her archly Martian detachment, Poddy defies a geocentric view of the universe, dead after Copernicus but not yet buried, so long as Earth still is taken as the end and be-all of human existence. "Men come and go, but earth abides" (Ecclesiastes I:4). With seeming naïveté, a teenage girl beholds our planetary home from out of some remote and alien part of the cosmos, in which it is not Earth that abides, but men—colonists expanding out there among the stars. Poddy's pioneering ancestors left good old Terra so long ago that she has only a garbled memory of its most elementary features. A place where water is over your head! That's all it's known for, this almost forgotten, used-up, desertable city, left behind to die of industrial pollution, human overpopulation, and unending warfare. In this, she slyly pronounces a Last Judgment on Terra's bad management, invoking the spectre of Bertrand Russell's "philosophic Martian biologist" who, in *Has Man a Future?*, visits a failed Earth to find a negative answer to that question.[18]

Heinlein's answer, of course, is positive. After Ralph Waldo Emerson, he describes himself as "a short term pessimist and a long term optimist." Or as Lazarus Long puts it, he is "Pessimist by policy, optimist by temperament. . . . This permits you to play out the game happily, untroubled by the certainty of the outcome" (*LL*, 352).

His Marsgirl, to be sure, offers a gloomy view of Earth's immediate fate. But his purpose is to do some Twain-like kicking of sacred cows, in this case a geocentric smugness that remains indifferent to the saving prospects of space travel. He looks to a secure human future in that direction, while kicking at the stalwart common sense of those who find such hope too visionary. He means in particular those in the U. S. Congress who would cut back on federal budgeting of NASA (National Aeronautical and Space Administration), for the sake of spending more on social programs—they, and their public constituents, who complain about "wasting all that money on stupid, useless space stunts when we have so many really important problems to solve right here on Earth" (*EU*, 504).

Poddy not only entertains with the ironical humor of her cosmic viewpoint, she also speaks for her author's Emersonian optimism. At heart, *Podkayne of Mars* is a tool of improvement and uplift in the old Puritan tradition. Disguising it as an entertainment, Heinlein writes as a public educator, aiming to cultivate in his readers a less parochial, more extraterrestrial-minded breed of world savers. "It is impossible to be a fan of my fiction and not be enthusiastic for space travel" (*EU*, 511).

Indeed, Heinlein's works are cited as references in technical publications of the Space Settlement Studies Project at Niagara University. This research project looks ahead to the human problems of designing permanent, large-scale habitats in Earth orbit or on the moon—the first steps to deep-space exploration and settlement. To questions about the legal, social, and political ordering of such off-Earth colonies, Heinlein (whose imagination goes well beyond the romance of rocketry) offers a fund of possible answers worth considering. (Who in this business can ignore even those passing allusions, in *The Cat Who Walks through Walls*, to "breathing fees" and "by-standers courts" on the Golden Rule space habitat?) More active as a pressure group is the L-5 Society, formed in 1975, "with the purpose of promoting space development in governmental . . . and private sectors." (L-5 is short for LaGrange libration point number five, an area of gravitational stability between Earth and moon that is ideal for locating the man-made, city-sized space habitats the Society envisions.) And here comes the point—the Society's members refer to themselves as "Heinlein's children."[19] Himself a member, and a subscriber to the *Commercial Space Report* (with its logo of a space-suited businessman carrying an attaché case), Heinlein is most vocal on the side of the private sector—this in keeping with his heroic American capitalist, D. D. Harriman, who initiated space flight in the Future History story, "The Man Who Sold the Moon." But it is Lazarus Long who has the last word on the virtues of free enterprise when he says, "Taxes are not levied for the benefit of the taxed" (*LL*, 250).

So much for Heinlein's optimistic outlook in the long term. But he has not failed to be helpful as well in coping with the dark problems of the short term. If Walt Whitman's "nation of nations" is to be made safe for undertaking its "kosmic destiny," it must meanwhile stay the hand of its fearsome adversary. Heinlein served as advisor to Lieutenant General Daniel O. Graham at the time he was preparing his position papers on Project High Frontiers. Submitted to President Ronald Reagan, this has now become national policy in the name of the Space Defense Initiative.

Finally, it is worth mentioning that both Twain and Heinlein are noted for their ailurophilia. To celebrate the 150th anniversary of Mark Twain's birth, the city of Elmira in November 1985 held a Festival of Cats. This in honor of the man who wrote, in Pudd'nhead Wilson's Calendar, "A home without a cat—and a well-fed, well-petted, and properly revered cat—may be a perfect home, perhaps, but how can it prove title?" By that measure, the Heinlein home has ever earned its title. Likewise does Lazarus Long have his notebook saying: "Anyone who considers protocol unimportant has never dealt with a cat" (*LL*, 350). Moreover, both authors are fond of turning similes on a close observation of cat behavior. In *The Innocents Abroad*, for example, Twain comes up with this anent the walk of a French dandy: "He stepped as gently and as daintily as a cat crossing a muddy street" (chap. 13). Heinlein's enterpreneur of space travel, D. D. Harriman, is "busy as a cat with two tails" (*PTT*, 205). In fact, Heinlein more than once borrows Twain's locution with reference to cramped quarters in which there is not room enough "to swing a cat" (e.g., in *The Rolling Stones*, 70); the allusion being to a sport so ugly that it may be made light of, in the lofty certainty that any cat-abuser is beyond the redemptive powers of a cat-petting moralist. "Where cat is, *is* civilization" *(Number of the Beast*, 333).

On the cover of *The Cat Who Walks through Walls* is a correct likeness of the author's cat Pixel, sitting on the heroine's shoulder, the hero standing close behind. Petronius the Arbiter, in *The Door into Summer*, is a former Heinlein cat in every behavioral detail. In *Cat*, Pete the character actor gives way to a full billing for Pixel in a title published, significantly, on the 150th anniversary of Twain's birth in 1985, and it contains at least three direct references to him (149, 237, 371). What this hints at is that Heinlein, contrary to what the critics hope to find, is more autobiographical about his cats than he is about his inner life. And why not? If he resists interpretation (by which he means a search for the man in his work), perhaps he has more to say in his texts than secrets to encode in them. Like Twain, he is forthright in his defense of the idea of personal freedom, as was the Roman goddess of liberty, standing in the Aventine Mount, who is portrayed holding a broken sceptre in her outstretched hand and with a cat lying at her feet—no other animal suggesting a greater enemy to all constraint. Or as Lazarus Long says, "Never try to out-stubborn a cat" (*LL*:350).

One difference, however, is worth underlining, if only to correct the false impression I may have given by highlighting Heinlein's address at the Naval Academy. He is not the habitual public speaker as was Twain. Indeed, he recoils from the idea of the writer as a celebrity. He lives a private life, and used to work up to eighteen hours a day for about eight or nine months of the year, then spend the summer on travel like any ordinary tourist, without calling attention to himself even when he went on exotic trips by unordinary means of transportation.

The Forrestal lecture he took on as a duty to his alma mater, once invited to speak there. The same goes for his few appearances at the SF conferences: loyalty to his readers. His critics find him reclusive and intolerant of his own following. But who more democratic than he? Or more American, the same thing in Walt Whitman's vocabulary.

Never a publicity seeker, whenever honored at such gatherings, Heinlein obliged, leaving the privacy of home and workshop to receive in person his hand-sculpted Hans Oberth rocket-ship trophies from his fans (not to mention his Grand Master Award of 1975 from his fellow SF writers, a galactic nebula embedded in a starry block of plastic), give thank-you speeches to the assembled crowds, and then sit down and autograph endless copies of his books for fans.

Whitman, who liked to identify himself with the democratic multitudes, addressed the reader as "friend and comrade." Yet no American writer ever did so in such a literal way in front of a whole gallery of friends and professional comrades than did the modest Heinlein at these conventions, some of them topping five thousand in attendance. These include three World Conferences in 1941, 1961, and 1976, to which he was invited as guest of honor; and the other five conferences he dutifully attended to receive Hugo awards in 1956, 1960, 1962, 1967; and then the award from his fellows in 1975—altogether a mark of unprecedented reader and professional elevation.

That Heinlein felt it his duty to attend these meetings is no case of false modesty. He simply practices the humanism he preaches, that private relationships are what makes life meaningful. Who said it better than George Garret in his novel, *Poison Pen, or: Live Now and Pay Later* (1986)? One of his characters has it that "public life is an illusion. Only private life is real and matters." So with Heinlein. It is for him a matter of honor and principle that he care for his domestic privacy against the blandishments of fame.

As further evidence of his position, consider this: No other science-fiction author (and perhaps no other living American author) nearly approaches Heinlein in commercial value when it comes to dealing on the secondhand market. Every one of his ordinary trade book titles is of supreme interest to collectors. Consult the catalogs of L. W. Currey, the world's largest rare book dealer in the SF field and its principal bibliographer, which reflect Heinlein's "astronomical distance" from the nearest competition.

Heinlein has no need to sell himself to sell his work. He labors at his craft, working as hard to entertain and instruct as he would have at military leadership, had he been able to follow that ambition. His work advertises itself because it is a good product. He has every right to be as retiring as Henry David Thoreau, the good pencil maker and woodsman, who left his writing desk at Walden Pond only to lecture by special invitation on the lyceum circuit, and who wrote, in "Life without Principle" (1863), "the aim of the laborer should be, not to get his living . . . but to perform a certain work."

That principle is Heinlein's too, as he long since has had no need to write for money. Not a little of it is demonstrated in the character of D. D. Harriman, his heroic capitalist, who is no crass bottom-liner after all. Asked, "How does a guy go about getting rich, like you did?," Harriman replies, "Getting rich? I can't say; I never tried to get rich, or well known or anything like that." Disbelief. Then: "No, I just wanted to live a long time and see it all happen" (*PTT*, 255). What he wanted to see happen, and what he brought about, was the advent of space travel. It was his "Wonderful Dream" (*PTT*, 170).

Chapter Two
The Fifty-Dollar Amateur Writer's Prize

After years of seeking literary fame, E. A. Poe finally hit it off with a science-fiction story, "Ms. Found in a Bottle" (1833), entered in a fifty-dollar prize contest run by the *Baltimore Saturday Visitor*. Poe won first prize for the best short story and fame as well.

Curiously enough, Heinlein got started by responding to a prize offer of the same amount, little more than a century later. But he was not looking to a literary career beforehand. His dream was the U. S. Naval Academy. Perhaps he admired his next older brother Rex, who had preceded him into Annapolis by some years. (But failing the eyesight requirement for naval service following his graduation from the Academy, Rex was commissioned in the army, ending up with the rank of colonel in charge of the electrical engineering department at West Point.)

At all events, young Robert was keen to follow; indeed, he might never have finished college had he not succeeded in getting into Annapolis. He was born in 1907 to a poor family in the little country town of Butler, Missouri, the third of seven children. Bam Lyle and Rex Ivar Heinlein, his parents, had not the means to provide a higher education following his graduation from Kansas City Central High School, where he was the top honors student of his class.

In 1924 he worked his way through one year at Kansas City Junior College, a local branch of the University of Missouri. By 1925 he got his Academy appointment on the strength of many good letters of recommendation. That a second member from the same family should be appointed so soon after the first is highly unusual and shows just how earnest the younger brother was in collecting his references. Robert Heinlein really wanted that appointment. Urging friends and employers to write letters on his behalf to Missouri Senator James A. Reed, he was proud to learn how well his effort paid off. "When I contacted the Senator's office, they said they had 100 letters—50 in my behalf, and one each for 50 other candidates." Unlike these other cases hanging on one important letter, he says, "my father had no political clout. I promoted myself by myself."

How much he really enjoyed Academy life is expressed in a science-fictionalized account of it in *Space Cadet,* the second title of his juvenile series. He was every bit the career officer, drawn as often from old American settlers from the mid-eighteenth century. (But another older brother made his way into the civil academy as a professor of political science.)

Graduating twentieth out of 243 in the class of 1929, Heinlein was able to serve the navy for only five years before his medical retirement. This returned him to civilian life and unemployment in 1934, during the Great Depression, as a tubercular patient supported only by his disability pay and by fantasies of more comfortable support on the perfect hospital bed. So he designed one, a water bed (his term), whose details are specified in *Stranger in a Strange Land,* and from which the maker of the first commercial version learned all he needed to know, without getting a patent on it. Every detail, drawn from spec-ifications in the novel, was judged by the courts to fall in the public domain, a tribute to Heinlein's technical realism. A story about his treatment as a bed patient during the 1930s is told in "No Bands Playing, No Flags Flying—" (*EU,* 238–43).

After his initial recovery he still was without a job. Picking up on his interest in physics and mathematics, he took graduate courses in these fields on the Los Angeles campus of the University of California, until a relapse obliged him to remove to Denver to recuperate. There he acquired a stake in two silver mines, the Sophia and the Shively lodes, under a bond-and-lease arrangement, but had the bad luck to lose his financial backer through death before the deal was closed. (Mark Twain had failed in the same business in Nevada.)

Returning to California, Heinlein entered the Democratic primary to unseat an incumbent assemblyman, losing by a close margin. Bad luck again; for as he says, "in politics there are no prizes for place or show" (*EU,* 4). He did, however, gain a lot of political savvy from that experience, of which he continues to make intelligent use in his fiction. Some tricks of the trade he improved on in his real-life campaign are related in "A Bathroom of Her Own" (*EU,* 245–66). It is his "Notorious Jumping Frog" story.

His insights into the political process are no less authentic when projected on the scale of solar-system statesmanship, as in *Double Star.* In one choice passage a supposed new ambassador to Mars (actually an actor playing the part) explains to his unversed confidant the virtues of a Farleyfile, which the narrator tells us is a method perfected by James A. Farley, President Roosevelt's political manager, "for handling the personal relations of politics." As it happens, this file was inherited by this actor assigned to double for the mysteriously missing Ambassador Bonforte; and as he learns to use it, we readers learn much as well. The narrator goes on:

It was nothing but a file about people. However, the art of politics is "nothing but" people. This file contained all, or most, of the thousands upon thousands of people Bonforte had met in the course of his long public life; each dossier consisted of what he knew about that person *from Bonforte's own personal contact.* Anything at all, no matter how trivial—in fact, trivia were always the first entries: names and nicknames of wives, children, and pets, hobbies, tastes in food or drinks, prejudices, eccentricities. Following this would be listed date and place and comments for *every occasion* on which Bonforte had talked to that particular man.[1]

The user of a Farleyfile has only to consult it for a minute or two before meeting the person in question. But the confidant to Bonforte's double thinks this altogether phony, dishonest, and insincere. No, comes back the rejoinder. "Do you apologize to your friend for caring so little about him that you can't simply remember his number?" These are the very things a politician "would like to remember if his memory were perfect. Since it isn't, it is no more phony to do it this way than it is to use a tickler file in order not to forget a friend's birthday— that's what it is: a giant tickler file to cover *anything.*" Then comes the real point of the lesson. No matter how important the statesman is relative to the person he meets, "the supremely important person in anyone's life is *himself*—and a politician must never forget that. So it is polite and friendly and warm-hearted to have a way to be able to remember about other people the sort of little things that they are likely to remember about him. It is also essential—in politics" (*DS,* 103f.).

This is the kind of worldly wisdom, savvy without cynicism, that makes Heinlein so instructive to his readers. The wit of the story itself is but the golden foil in which the jewel-like lessons are enwrapped and set. It is for these little lectures, aptly worked into the story line without halting it, that his fans revere him as their spiritual father. Or better, he is their straight-talking Dutch uncle.

Not that they learn from Bonforte how to be politicians. Everyday
life has its own need for diplomacy. In Heinlein's next-to-last novel its
hero of senatorial rank speaks of his political enemy as an adversary
whose "intention is to get me angry, ruin my judgment, and get me
to make threats that I can't carry out." This adversary "was trying
hard to get my goat. So above all I must not let it happen" (*Cat*,
47f.). The lesson is useful even to us non-senators. Good form is
everything. A guest of the senator is killed while eating at his table,
very bad form on the part of his enemy. "The putative offense of
murder is not my concern," he says, but the crime of bad manners is.
"I must find the oaf who did this thing, explain to him his offense,
give him a chance to apologize, and kill him" (*Cat*, 36f.). If the reader
detects in this a later version of Edmund Spenser's chivalric attitude
toward life, which in *The Faerie Queene* (1590) states (in effect) that
the manners are the morals, the reader is not mistaken. That Heinlein
should find his main object of culture criticism in a declining respect
for the traditional values of politesse is, in fact, the one thing above
all that moves his modernist critics to tag him as a "reactionary."

In the event, this murder goes unresolved. But Heinlein characters
do not weep in their cups over Virgil's *lacrima rerum*, "the tears in
things." If they do, as does the lachrymose owner of Pete in *The Door
into Summer,* they have the fortitude to recover. So does the strangely
tortured hero of *Job.* He is forced by impossible changes in his world
to address all the basic questions: "We don't know who we are, or
where we come from, or why we are here." His being thrust into a
series of parallel worlds only calls attention to the same old troublesome
worries of his original life. The impossible thing is everybody's thing.
Only now, however, is he ready "to face the ancient mystery of life,
untroubled by my inability to solve it." No more retreat into drink.
"I had sobered up so much that I now realized that I not only could
not solve my problems through spirits but must shun alchohol until I
did solve them." But for Heinlein fans this does not come across as
the abstract moralizing of a faded religious faith. It persuades with
avuncular horse sense: "for pragmatic reasons virtue should rule even
when moral instruction has ceased to bind" (*Job*, 54, 67). Responsible
selfhood means holding to one's powers of judgment without metaphysical angst.

Such is Heinlein's authority to teach and persuade, earned after a
half century of writing. But he did not begin until five years after his
medical retirement from the navy in 1934.

By early 1939, Heinlein had yet to write his first story. Following his "disastrous" political campaign in California, he was flat broke and with a mortgage to pay. Retired at twenty-seven, only one year short of the age at which the tubercular Stephen Crane died, he did not find his new career until he was thirty-two.

Pushed to the wall by his business and political failures, but spared a new onset of his illness, Heinlein's eye caught the announcement of a fifty-dollar-prize contest offered by *Thrilling Wonder Stories* for the best amateur short story by an unpublished writer. As he notes, in the Depression year of 1939, "one could fill three station wagons with fifty dollars worth of groceries" (*EU*, 4).

This prize offer, however, did not catch his eye quite by accident. Once he learned about science fiction in his boyhood, he always enjoyed reading it thereafter. How he came upon it is related in the following anecdote. At the age of sixteen (in 1923), as he tells it, he took a trip from his home in Butler, Mo., to do some mountain climbing in Colorado. With only a small amount of cash left over for food to eat on the train back, in the magazine stand at the railway station he spotted a title that he bought and read with immediate interest. This was the August 1923 issue of *Science and Invention* (from 1920), the special "scientific fiction" number that foreshadowed the name "science fiction." The purchase left him with pennies in change for a few doughnuts. Formerly the *Electrical Experimenter* (from 1914), the magazine used to run the occasional science-fiction story, a policy success that led its publisher Hugo Gernsback (after whom the Hugo Awards are named) to initiate *Amazing Stories* in 1926, a whole magazine given to such like. The first of the science-fiction pulps, it was imitated from the start in drawing upon every synonym for "amazing" to be found in Roget's *Thesaurus,* including *Astounding Stories* from 1930. This is the magazine Heinlein began in, after it became *Astounding Science-Fiction* (*ASF* to its fans).

The prize offer appeared, however, in *Thrilling Wonder Stories.* After four days of concentrated effort Heinlein turned out his first story, "Life-Line." But the contest advertisement only suggested the idea of writing; and he sent the story instead to *Collier's* in the belief that, far from pulpish, the story was well suited to such a general magazine then reaching circulation of two and a half million. *Collier's* bounced it (their mistake), so Heinlein considered the prize offer. But he had another idea. The story came to seven thousand words. At one cent a word, paid by the top magazine in the field, *Astounding Science-Fiction,* that amounted to seventy dollars—twenty more than offered in prize money, twenty dollars more for groceries. So he sent "Life-Line" to *ASF*. Its editor, John W. Campbell, bought it and asked for more. Thereafter Heinlein became *ASF*'s largest supplier of copy, providing twenty percent of it by 1941. Finally, he paid off his mortgage. Then World War II started, and for the duration Heinlein wrote nothing but technical monographs.

He had returned to the service as a civilian engineer for the U. S. Naval Air Experimental Station at Mustin Field in Philadelphia. Working with him, at his instance, were two other technically trained *ASF* writers, Isaac Asimov (a biochemist) and L. Sprague de Camp (a mechanical engineer). The latter was appointed to head the high-altitude laboratory, where he and Heinlein developed pressure suits—prototypical space suits—complete with fishbowl helmets made of lucite. If the space suits worn by today's astronauts look like those depicted in old science-fiction magazines, it is because they were invented by science-fiction writers themselves.[2]

It was here at Mustin Field that Heinlein met Navy Lieutenant Virginia Gerstenfeld ("Ginny"), a chemist and aeronautical testing engineer, whom he married in 1948 and whose certificate of service is displayed over his word processor. Like Mark Twain's wife, she is his primary editor, and she helps with the research and handles the voluminous fan mail, not to say the business accounts. "Her brain is a great help to me professionally" (*EU,* 520). She also does the homework in preparing for their summer vacations, which, Heinlein explains, have included visits to "more than sixty countries on six continents, by freight ship, helicopter, dog sled, safari, jet plane, mule back, canal boat, etc." (*EU,* 422). For example, she spent two years learning Russian in advance of their trip to the Soviet Union in 1950. Returning home, she wrote up a report, as she did on all their trips, with one copy for the research files and others for family friends.[3]

When I visited the Heinleins, they had just returned from the Antarctic, one of the last few places on earth they had not previously visited. (If Heinlein takes a global view of things, it is because he really knows his planet!) At the same time, I could not help noticing something more subtly helpful on Ginny's part—her half of their routine diurnal conversation. Its intelligent byplay is echoed in the dialogue of Heinlein's competent heroes and heroines, as in that passing between the bright teenagers of his juveniles.

Heinlein's chief monograph from his wartime service is *Testing in Connection with the Development of Strong Plastics for Aircraft* (Philadelphia: Naval Air Materials Center, 1944). This is based on his own plastics research into the qualities of methylmethacrylate (lucite or plexiglass), then under development for warplane canopies and bubble turrets, as for pressure-suit helmets. Were this obscure government document to be republished today ("It's written in English," he is proud to say), it would stand as a good model of technical writing in university programs just now beginning (as at Illinois Tech) to take this up as a teachable skill—one no less important to the Space Age than the ability to invent new hardware.

Not that Heinlein's time-out from writing science fiction subtracted from his literary development. Quite the contrary. The skills of technical exposition that he learned in writing his engineering reports he later applied especially to his boy's and girl's books. In each one of them is a witty little technical lecture on how things work. What makes them witty, however, is just the reverse of what is wanted in a technical monograph, which is not only to elucidate but to familiarize. These little essays elucidate, to be sure; but their intent is rather to defamiliarize. By "making strange," in a sophisticated use of humorous irony, their instructive effect is actually enhanced.

A good example comes from *The Rolling Stones,* in which the technology of the reciprocating engine powering the automobile is explained in such a way. The excuse for doing so is a retrospective look at the "mechanical buffoonery" of our primitive road machines, viewed from a future stage of "proper design." The narrator goes on:

A reciprocating engine was a collection of miniature heat engines using (in a basically inefficient cycle) a small percentage of an exothermic chemical reaction, a reaction that was started and stopped every split second. Much of the heat was intentionally thrown away into a "water jacket" or "cooling system," then wasted into the atmosphere through a heat exchanger.

What little was left caused blocks of metal to thump foolishly back and forth (hence the name "reciprocating") and thence through a linkage to cause a shaft and flywheel to spin around. The flywheel (believe it if you can) had no gyroscopic function; it was used to store kinetic energy in a futile effort to cover up the sins of reciprocation. The shaft at long last caused the wheels to turn and thereby propelled this pile of junk over the countryside.[4]

Not only mechanical subjects are treated to this kind of exposition. Even more remarkable is the essay on the basics of mental health, most

useful to adolescent readers, in *Time for the Stars* (chap. 9). Small
wonder that youthful Heinlein fans have the least use of any teenagers
for school psychologists.

A letter from a former student, now a research engineer with the
Association of American Railroads, in its Technical Center here on the
campus of Illinois Institute of Technology, suggests the kind of influence
that Heinlein does indeed have on his readers. Having discovered the
Heinlein juveniles at age ten, he says of them,

they were the first books that I ever read completely on my own without
any prompting or necessity—and I loved them.

In these books, I became aware of intelligent, competent, exemplary people
who were really unlike anyone in my environment. I admired Heinlein's
people and they served as "role models" for me. I really wanted to be like
them! And, in a sense, Heinlein told me *how* I could be like them! He laid
before me, in his books, a blueprint, a roadmap in the following way:

I suppose that I had a latent talent for mathematics, science and engineering
all along. But Heinlein showed me how to get from where I was to where
I wanted to be, especially in mathematics. There was no one around me in
my grammar school environment who could have told me what sequence to
follow, or who could have made the applications of mathematics seem so
exciting. But, through Heinlein's books, I knew how to proceed, and I was
excited about reaching each level: algebra, geometry, trigonometry, analytic
geometry, calculus, differential equations, vector analysis, and so on. During
this period, I would re-read my favorite Heinlein books and compare my
progress with his "blueprint." And, best of all, Heinlein indicated that, if
I mastered mathematics, all the other fields of science and engineering would
be within my grasp.

I was especially impressed, in *The Rolling Stones* [Chap. 4], by Mr. Stone's
lecture to his twin boys before the family took off on their odyssey through
the Solar System. On a screen, he projected a list of the fields of mathematics.
The boys were familiar only with the subjects up through calculus he displayed
in the upper left hand corner of the screen—they knew how to "count on
their fingers" with that kind of applied math, but their father wanted them
to go beyond engineering to learn how to "think mathematically." During
the trip through the Solar System, we are kept abreast of how the boys
progress in their study of formal mathematics. To me, this aspect of the
book was as exciting as the story itself.[5]

Such is one measure of Heinlein's instructive influence. But it all
began in the prewar issues of *ASF*, with his Future History stories.
With these, Heinlein from 1939 projected the historical lessons of our
nation's founding onto a wider human future enlightened by the same
moral, spiritual, and political ideals.

Chapter Three
History to Come: New Frontiers

In Heinlein's future history of space travel it is the Americans who lead the way by replaying the adventure of Columbus and the voyage of the Pilgrims. The first flight of discovery to the moon (in "The Man Who Sold the Moon") is by the spaceship *Santa Maria* (differently named the *Lunatic* in a related story, "Requiem"), followed by the *Mayflower* whose crew founded the first human colony there, Luna City. These are ships built by D. D. Harriman. In financing them, he opens up the "new frontiers" of outer space (*PTT*, 192). From the moon, deep space is pioneered in starships, those "covered wagons of the galaxy" (*TEL*, 300). The first of these, a failed experiment, is the *Vanguard* (in "Universe"). But its sister ship, *New Frontiers*, not only reaches the planets of another star system, it returns with knowledge of other intelligent beings out there *(Methuselah's Children)*. Superior to humans in their technology, and seemingly stronger in their despotic socialism, they test mankind's right to expand outward, its very right to exist in the same universe. But as ever, any frontier is the only valid proving ground of freedom's worth.

The omnibus edition of Heinlein's Future History stories is *The Past through Tomorrow (PTT)*. This title is subtle in the extreme. At the more obvious level, it evokes the American past as a guide to humanity's future, leading on, somewhen in a later century, to "The First Human Civilization" (see Future History chart in *PTT*, 660f., righthand column). The makers of tomorrow belong to Walt Whitman's nation of nations. The United States is the planet's cosmic hope, or, as Emerson said, America is "the country of the Future." It is destined to open up those open-ended new frontiers beyond all closing, for the everlasting survival of the human species, given the dynamics of its population growth (a Darwinian fact of life that Whitman well appreciated in his short essay, "Darwinism," in *Specimen Days*). Expand or die. Suffocate in cradle earth outgrown, or move outward. "Our race will spread out through space—unlimited room, unlimited energy, unlimited wealth. This is certain" (*EU*, 502).

Yet Heinlein takes the conservative position, as opposed to a radical futurism, that certain truths from the past, embodied in the American experience, are forever settled. As William F. Buckley, Jr., puts it, "Whatever is to come cannot outweigh the importance to man of what has gone before."[1] That is the subtle meaning of Heinlein's title: tomorrow will be made through the past, as the best of it runs through American history, or it will not be made in any liberating way at all.

Three and one half centuries before Apollo 11 landed astronauts Armstrong and Aldrin on the moon (following much congressional debate over the merits of funding NASA for such a stupid space stunt) William Bradford in his classic of colonial literature, *Of Plimoth Plantation,* reported how the Pilgrims debated their uncertain voyage to America. In chapter 6 he tells how the proposed voyage

raised many variable opinions amongst men, and caused many doubts and fears among them selves. Some, from their reasons and hop[e]s conceived, laboured to stir up and incourage the rest to undertake and prosecute the same; others, againe, out of their fears, objected against it, and sought to divert from it, aledging many things, and those neither unreasonable nor unprobable. . . .

It was answered, that all great, and honourable actions are accompanied with great difficulties, and must be enterprised and overcome with unanswerable courages.

Like the Apollo astronauts, our Puritan ancestors had "the Right Stuff," to borrow the title of Tom Wolfe's 1979 book, itself a modern classic of bravery and courage.

The Right Stuff is a near-novelized account of the Mercury astronauts and their training program, done in a naturalistic style so hyped-up in a good-humored way that the effect is altogether uplifting—or should one say transcendental? While watching the 1983 film based on it, I said to myself, "Wowie, if this isn't the best SF flick ever!" But no; it was the real thing in every human and technical particular, vastly more entertaining than empty fantasies like *Star Wars.* But for a while there I was transfixed by the illusion that I was watching Heinlein brought to the screen, he is that much the realist of the romantic.

At all events, Heinlein's space mission, like the voyage of our Pilgrim forefathers to the New World and its unknown future, is more than just a migration. For our ancestors, it was an exodus divinely ordained. As Moses led the Israelites out of slavery in Egypt, so did the Pilgrims bring themselves to America away from bondage to the medieval past of the unfree Old World. Harriman's *Santa Maria* is a rechristened space shuttle, formerly the *Care Free*. Under that name it had served to safely maintain nuclear power plants in Earth orbit, where atomic fuel is generated for the *Santa Maria*. As Harriman watches it lift off, one of his associates remarks, "He looks as Moses must have looked, when he gazed out over the promised land" (*PTT*, 212).

But more. These orbiting power plants, their energy transmitted by radio beams, are Harriman's answer to the hazards of atomic energy. When all others in the nuclear industry failed to control its dangers, he personally took responsibility for it, acting on the Puritan's faith in one's individual ability to overcome the most insurmountable of obstacles (see "Blow Ups Happen" in *PTT*, 73–120).

The translator of Alexis de Tocqueville's *Democracy in America* (1835; tr. 1838) found it necessary to coin a new word for the quality of men his French author found in this country, the secret of its political and business success. And that word, occurring in English for the first time, is "individualism."[2] It is what Emerson codified in his doctrine of self-reliance, and what Heinlein speaks to directly when he has Lazarus Long say, "The greatest productive force is human selfishness" (*LL*, 349), although this meaning is frequently mistaken. But Heinlein does no more than answer the question posed by Hector St. John de Crèvecœur when, in *Letters from an American Farmer* (1872), he asked, "What is an American?" Fully in tune with Lazarus Long's notebook saying, de Crèvecœur answers that "the American is a new man, who acts on new principles." Here in America the rewards of a man's work follow "with equal steps the progress of his labor; his labor is founded on the basis of nature, *self-interest*." Thus, "Here we have in some measure regained the ancient dignity of our species." It is that pristine dignity, no less, that Heinlein heroes are given to upholding in their every adventure.

Today, somehow, Emerson's transcendentalist thought often is cited for its denial of self-reliance when it comes to the self-interests of commerce. This is incorrect; Emerson is by no means anticapitalist. He says rather that America is "the country of the Future" precisely because of its being so much a business country. Its "business ethics" make for the public good, standing as a bulwark against the abuses of government and its malign tendency to make war. Trade makes for a "beneficent tendency." It is "a plant which grows wherever there is peace. . . . It is a new agent in the world, and one of great function; it is a very intellectual force."[3] So it is with the venture capitalism of D. D. Harriman in Heinlein's work.

Harriman pioneers the moon for private-profit capitalism and for peace, so as to shut out any claims to it by the other super power. That, too, is part of the Wonderful Dream; and he himself takes full responsibility for its outcome. Were either side allowed to lay claim to the moon for the purpose of building military bases on it, Harriman tells his associates, "presently there will be the God-damndest war this planet has ever seen—and we'll be to blame" (*PTT,* 146). Once his captain lands and returns the *Santa Maria,* he is asked to make a statement to the press.

Tell them that this is the beginning of the human race's greatest era. Tell them that every one of them will have a chance to follow in Captain LeCroix's footsteps, seek out new planets, wrest a home for themselves in new lands. Tell them that it means new frontiers, a shot in the arm for prosperity. It means—. (*PTT,* 191f.).

The rest goes unstated. But it is explained in the Future History chart. With the advent of Harriman's Lunar Corporations, there begins, after an era of statist controls, "a return to nineteenth-century economy" (*PTT,* 661).

Of course, that bit about everyone having a chance to homestead new worlds implies a selective process. Heinlein's future history of the American journey *from* America by spaceship follows on the frontier journey *within* America by wagon train and, before that, the equally daring journey *to* America by deep-water sailing ship. The men and women destined to pioneer the new frontiers of outer space in those "covered wagons of the galaxy" will be self-selected for the right stuff, no less than were their heroic ancestors. Or looked at another way, Heinlein's history to come is a moral lesson reminding the reader of our nation's founding idealism, the better to inform (and reform) the present—"the past through tomorrow."

It is a misreading of him, however, to find in his breed of frontiersmen a case for "rugged individualism," a phrase recurring in the critical literature. In at least one instance the adjective is "wolfish" individualism.[4] This is not far from what the Marxists call "bourgeois individualism." But always the sinister implication is that Heinlein stands for an irresponsible, antisocial brand of self-interest. Indeed, this altogether typical critique comes down to one invariable indictment, that Heinlein takes a doctrinal stance on behalf of social Darwinism.

Now it is true that Heinlein writes of *Homo sapiens* as a Darwinian species. At one level of storytelling, not his only one, he does treat man as a planetary organism having a biological destiny above and beyond that of the individuals that comprise humankind. But it does not follow that he is a social Darwinist, and all that implies for economic warfare battled out within the species for the sake of its top dogs, as if man were just another animal.

This being the key issue around which the interpretation of his work revolves, I brought it up to Heinlein during my visit, and he replied with some heat. Such a line of criticism he takes as more than mere error—it is "accusation." And he is right to so respond. He did not pledge his life, when he entered upon the military profession, to defend the freedoms of American democracy if these are defined as antisocial liberties. He did not prepare to die for economic individualism.

In fact, Lazarus Long has it that a self-reliant person should be able to "cooperate, act alone," as the occasion demands. And more. The full text of this saying goes as follows.

A human being should be able to change a diaper, plan an invasion, butcher a hog, conn a ship, design a building, write a sonnet, balance accounts, build a wall, set a bone, comfort the dying, take orders, give orders, cooperate, act alone, solve equations, analyze a new problem, pitch manure, program a computer, cook a tasty meal, fight efficiently, die gallantly. Specialization is for insects. (*LL,* 248).

These clearly are the virtues of de Crèvecœur's new man, the American who acts on new principles; what Walt Whitman celebrated as democratic individualism in similar lines from "Myself and Mine" (1881).

> Myself and mine gymnastic ever,
> To stand the cold or heat, to take good aim with
> a gun, to sail a boat, to manage horses, to
> begat superb children.
> To speak readily and clearly, to feel at home
> among common people,
> And to hold our own in terrible positions on
> land and sea.

The self-reliant American democrat is a responsible man, and a responsible person is omnicompetent, or "gymnastic"—the essential quality of the frontiersmen.

Heinlein's D. D. Harriman is cut from the same cloth. He started out with a small family business, only to enlarge it until it becomes Harriman Enterprises, a global empire of interlocking corporations. The difference is, he runs this whole huge thing as a personal extension of himself; he is not one of a faceless lot of portfolio managers of the bureaucratic sort that put the struggling hero of a story called "Let There Be Light" out of business. Heinlein's complaint is that the executives of today's "corpocracy" don't work as hard as did the robber barons of the nineteenth century. None of them have Harriman's pioneering spirit and risk-taking zeal, much less his imagination to dream of new and better good works.

Indeed, heroic capitalism is the very theme of Heinlein's first story, "Life-Line." A Dr. Pinero invents a length-of-life predicting machine that threatens the established insurance industry. Its actuarial methods now are outdated; so its political lawyers bring this creative little man to court, demanding that his innovative product be taken off the market. But the judge, a Heinlein viewpoint character, denounces their "strange doctrine [that because a] corporation has made a profit out of the public for a number of years, the government and the courts are charged with the duty of guaranteeing such profit in the future, even in the face of changing circumstances and contrary to public interest." He denies their demand "that the clock of history be stopped, or turned back, for their private benefit" (*PTT*, 28).

But not even Harriman is above shady dealing. "If we have to, we should buy the judge" (*PTT*, 127). If that's what it takes for Harriman tycoonery to get the job done, that's permitted because Harriman Enterprises do the right thing for the right purpose. The moral difference is everything. D. D. Harriman pioneers the moon out of the bravery of his venture capitalism; the risk is his for the making of profits on a grand scale of unprecedented daring. At the same time, he acts as an agent of human destiny, opening up those "new frontiers" for the general good. This is to the purpose of Emerson's business ethics in this truly progressive nation of nations.

As happened in real life, the industrialists who built spaceships for the Apollo program did so under government contract, not as Harriman did it by means of private enterprise. All the same it was not a federally funded rocketship that achieved the first lunar landing; it was the astronauts, those men of unanswerable courages. And in due time, as Heinlein rightly supposes, the same type of men (and women) will colonize the moon.

In "The Black Pits of Luna," one of the *Saturday Evening Post* stories Heinlein wrote in his immediate postwar period, a group of silly "dirtside" tourists visit the Luna City of Harriman's founding. Taking a space-suited tour among the craters of its environs, they go hysterical when a small boy gets lost—a brat impossible to discipline and underaged as well for this trip, according to regulations. But his father has political connections powerful enough to demand of the tour guides that the rules be waived in this case. When the boy is discovered missing, his mother cries for bloodhounds(!), and his father meekly surrenders to her idiotic demand, even though he knows better. All the other tourists are equally helpless and useless in this crisis. Only the boy's older brother, the narrator, keeps his head and finds the boy.

The comic element in the story recalls a vein of humor discovered by Bret Harte (or rediscovered by him after Augustus Baldwin Longstreet, James Fenimore Cooper, and William Gilmore Simms, and before Twain's polished reworking of it), in the collision of the cultured and the primitive on the advancing American frontier. Heinlein himself called Bret Harte to my attention when he advised me to visit the nearby locale of "The Luck of Roaring Camp." Reflecting on the scene, I came to see that Heinlein's humor is well rooted in a native tradition that finds comedy in the primitive frontiersman turning out to be, at heart, the more cultured of the two parties when they collide.

After the undeserving boy is saved, yet saved for all that, the guide admonishes his parents: "Stay off the moon. You don't belong here; you're not the pioneering type." But the narrator confides in him, "I just wanted to tell you that I'll be back, if you don't mind." And the guide, recognizing one of his own, shakes hands with him and says, "I know you will, Shorty" (*PTT,* 299f.).

This boy has the right stuff, the same that is selected for in *Citizen of the Galaxy,* one of the juvenile books, where it is advised, "get the lad to any frontier world, where a brain and a willingness to work were all a man needed" (32). That's how men are made out of boys, or at least some boys; and the lesson is even more harshly drawn in *Tunnel in the Sky,* another story of juvenile heroism in which a saving youth rescues his fellow boys and girls from the perils of isolation in a field test of survival training gone wrong. How unlike the equal leveling down to savagery that William Golding portrays in *Lord of the Flies* (1954). And for that pessimistic fantasy about the limits of human nature, Golding won the Nobel Prize for Literature. Heinlein's realism about unequal differences in the human makeup is not the sort of thing recognized in such literary prizes; but he is the better teacher to his many more readers. As Lazarus Long says, "All men are created unequal," a fact of life that is bound to assert itself in light of his related saying, "Natural laws have no pity" (*LL*, 243, 351).

The moon is an outpost of Heinlein's new frontiers, a hazardous environment even within the airlocked confines of Luna City, where quick reactions to every blowout, caused by mechanical failure in the buried deeps or by meteoroids crashing on some crucial surface feature, are normal to a routine living with unexpected danger. Not wild beasts or hostile Indians as on the old frontier, there are none of these on the moon, but there is all the same an untamed wilderness thereon to be exploited by the same daring—and something more. Here, where technical expertise of a high order counts for survival, tenacious individualism combines with professional cooperation to make a go of it, bringing out the best of the human potential in all of its unequal diversity. The frontier, as ever, selects for competence in its relentless and remorseless natural way. The title of a later Heinlein novel tells it all: *The Moon is a Harsh Mistress.* The moon's colonists are "moonies," a different breed of men and women; and while they excel in unique capabilities for the good of their own self-culture, they also serve the generality of mankind by opening up a new and open-ended frontier for unlimited racial expansion and human progress. Each one is a "Loony at heart." In a word, they are "moonstruck," his or her spiritual mark of grace so named in a related story, "It's Great to be Back!" (*PTT*, 316f.).

In time, the moon develops its own industries for export to Earth, this in addition to serving as a way station for deep-space exploration and colonization. Now economically independent, it declares political independence on 4 July 2076, in a new American Revolution. By then, however, the moon had attracted immigrants from all nations, as had America from the start. The moonstruck Loonies who declare lunar independence are drawn from all races and national cultures, and it is they who replay the American experience and the American Revolution of 1776.

As America was that last best hope on earth for the best national idea, so now the moon is the last best hope for the continued survival of man as a biological species, now that the old terrestrial homeland slowly fades into a sunset decline (after World War III), following its inability to control war, overpopulation, and famine. Those who are moonstruck are a special breed of frontiersman, to be sure. They show the way to the human future, out there among the stars, in a wider universe no less hostile than any place conquered by people with the right stuff here on Sol III. But there is no need for any planning authority to design this outcome; the future course of racial progress takes care of itself. The moonies and their far-flung descendants, traveling in their starships, those "covered wagons of the galaxy," are self-selecting. There is no need to improve the breed for its reluctant salvation by any program of positive eugenics.

Again, as Lazarus Long says, "Natural laws have no pity." They do their work unaided, without the help of any techniques of artificial genetic selection that may well lie in the powers of science in future to decide, as in the cynical view of that possibility given by Aldous Huxley in his *Brave New World* (1932). Heinlein will have none of this. For him, such a prospect is out of the question. He once played with the idea, only to dismiss it, in *Beyond This Horizon*. This novel of 1948 (serialized 1942) pictures a failed utopia of genetic engineering. Its "Great Research" (a phrase echoing the title of a 1915 Wells novel, *The Research Magnificent*) into the matter of how to plan for the breeding of survival types ends in the conclusion that man is after all a wild animal, incapable of domestication for any purpose whatsoever. "Survival! What for?" is the unanswerable question (*Beyond This Horizon*, 33).

Life is life, says Heinlein; "left to our own resources, improvement in the breed must come the hard way . . . and we will still remain wild animals" (*EU*, 383). Human destiny is whatever its pioneer types choose to bring to it, in keeping with the natural laws of the cosmos. The purpose of space travel is not to relieve the overpopulation of Earth, but to select yet again a new set of voyagers to another New World, this one unending in its openness to racial improvement, and for the betterment of all those individual lives who undertake it. And thus onward to the making of a new and better galactic civilization on the American model. Onward to the First Human Civilization.

Chapter Four
Other Voices, Other Rooms

For Henry James, the "celebrated distinction between the novel [of realism] and the romance" was pointless. He found such a "clumsy separation [to] have been made by critics and readers for their own convenience," although in fact they "have little reality or interest for the producer, from whose point of view it is of course that we are attempting to consider the art of fiction."[1]

James is exactly right. Fiction is all one to the writer, if not to his readers, much less to his publishers, who in the genre-regarding days of the pulp magazines went out of their way to go against the artistic unity of it all.

Heinlein ran into this taxonomic problem from the start. For example, when in the second year of writing he submitted to *Astounding Science-Fiction* his first fantasy story, "The Devil Makes the Law" (anthologized as "Magic, Inc." in *Waldo and Magic, Inc.*), his editor John Campbell shunted it over to the September 1940 issue of *Unknown Worlds,* a fantasy magazine run as a companion to his *ASF,* the real thing in science fiction; fantasy being a kind of poor cousin to science fiction in those days. Different magazines for different genres, ranked by worth, were the rule in the pulp magazine trade.

As a matter of fact, it was a fantasy magazine, *Weird Tales* (from 1923), that preceded the first of the science-fiction pulps. Its most famous regular contributors were H. P. Lovecraft and Ray Bradbury, not the sort of writers to appear in the pages of *ASF,* which came to be the top magazine in the American romantic underground; mainly because it above all others approached the mainstream standards of historical veracity. (Well . . . Bradbury did have one story, "Doodad," in the September 1943 issue of *ASF,* but that was his first and last one there, before he got his footing in *Weird Tales.*) Its fans always regarded it as the home of "hard core SF" (engineering fiction), the opposite of fantasy as they understood it from the artificial distinctions made by the magazine publishers themselves.

(*Weird Tales,* by the way, is a good example of how an unassuming aspect of American literature got itself twisted into a paraliterature of the specialty magazines. What made it pulpish was its concentration on second-rate spin-offs from the ghost and horror stories of Ambrose Bierce, once published in the general circulation magazines. Now they had their own bad imitations, written by H. P. Lovecraft et al. Heinlein's playful treatment of this half-baked subgenre is "Lost Legion," in which Ambrose Bierce himself figures.)

Looking back on "The Devil Makes the Law," it is hard to see why such distinctions were maintained. Yet fans vibrated either to science fiction or to fantasy, and there were plenty of specialty pulps to feed their special appetites. All the same Heinlein's contribution to *Unknown Worlds* was nothing if not historical in its true-to-life veracity. Here is to be found the same waggish insights into how the real world works that he delivers in his hard-core stuff. In this case he supplies a tough look at Chicago politics, as if its gangster elements were engaged in a supernatural protection racket, muscling in on legitimate business enterprises aided only by fair magical practices. It is a story of authentic culture criticism, its fantastic premise aside.

But artistic unities were not recognized in the diverse market Heinlein was obliged to sell to. He himself, the producer of his own fiction, always regarded the difference between fantasy and science fiction as pointless within the romance as James's disregard for the difference between romance and realism. Indeed, Heinlein has his own comment on this matter. It is his essay, "On the Writing of Speculative Fiction."[2] Here he conflates fantasy and science fiction, pulling it all under the science-fiction heading, whose initials, SF, he takes to stand for what he does in his own variety, namely Speculative Fiction. It is the same to him, hard-core science fiction or fantasy; all of it belongs to literature, realistic or romantic, as he has demonstrated in his versatile examples.

But it was not so easy to show off in the subdivided market wherein he began. Indeed, even within the covers of *ASF,* where he started with his Future History stories, it was editorial policy to separate these from another set of hard-core science-fiction stories that did not belong to this other series. Even this distinction had to be defined as the product of another author, under the pseudonym of Anson MacDonald. It was Robert A. Heinlein who had begun the Future History canon in *ASF,* with stories like "Life-Line" (August 1939). "Misfit" (November 1939), "Requiem" (January 1940), "The Roads Must Roll" (June 1940), "Coventry" (July 1940), "Blowups Happen" (September 1940), " '—And He Built a Crooked House—' " (February 1941), "Logic of Empire" (March 1941), "Universe" (May 1941), "Methuselah's Children" (July, August, September 1941), and "Common Sense" (October 1941, a sequel to "Universe").

Within many of these very same issues of *ASF* there appeared the alternative-world stories of Anson MacDonald, like "Sixth Column" (January, February, March 1941), "Solution Unsatisfactory" (May 1941), " '—We Also Walk Dogs' " (July 1941), "By His Bootstraps" (October 1941), "Goldfish Bowl" (March 1942), "Beyond This Horizon" (April, May 1942), and "Waldo" (August 1942).

"Waldo" was the last story Heinlein wrote before he returned to service, within twenty-four hours after the bombing of Pearl Harbor. But the editorial fiction that Heinlein and MacDonald were two different authors was kept up to the end, with Campbell's announcement that both men (who had tied for first place in reader polls throughout the prewar period) had returned to the navy at the same time (see *ASF*, February 1942, 35). Such were the fine genre distinctions in those pulpish days when, even within one magazine, the followers of Heinlein's Future History stories had their fanship safeguarded from the knowledge that stories outside that canon were written by the selfsame author. Today Heinlein is able to declare everything under his own name, in his numerous reprint collections.

But in his magazine days he used pseudonyms other than Anson MacDonald. Lyle Monroe, for example, seems to be a byline attached to lesser stories in lesser science-fiction magazines, as with "Lost Legion" (*Super Science Stories*, November 1941), "My Object All Sublime" (*Future*, February 1942), and "Pied Piper" (*Astonishing Stories*, May 1947). Also by Lyle Monroe is "Columbus was a Dope" (*Startling Stories*, May 1947), which properly belongs to the Future History canon; although it does not appear in *PTT*, the so-called omnibus edition of these stories. Then again, four other stories belonging to the canon also are missing. One of these is "Let There be Light," likewise by Lyle Monroe in one of the lesser magazines (*Super Science Stories*, May 1940). The others, under the Heinlein byline in *ASF* as already mentioned, are "Universe," "Common Sense," and " '—And He Built a Crooked House—.' " Their omission from *PTT* may be an oversight of the publisher, who advertised it as Heinlein's "Future History Stories: Complete in One Volume." Or maybe the author himself reconsidered, his privilege. Even so, it is confusing to find that, while these titles are edited out of the revised Future History chart, some of their characters are not (see *PTT*, 660, under list of "Characters" in the second column from the left). You will see there the names Douglass and Martin, inventors of the "Douglass-Martin sun-power-screens" (third column from the left under "Technical Data"), whereas the story in which they appear, "Let There Be Light," is expunged under the column headed "Stories." (The chart's revision, however, is not Heinlein's but the publisher's.)

Another pseudonym, used only once, is Caleb Saunders, for "Elsewhere" (anthologized as "Elsewhen" in *Assignment in Eternity*). Appearing in the September 1941 issue of *ASF*, it is neither a Future History story nor an equivalent "hard-core" science-fiction story of the sort done by Anson MacDonald. It is fantasy, or very close to that, being a metaphysical tale of time-and-space travel to a number of parallel worlds by an act of will and mental concentration. The universe has many mansions, and our world is but one room in that multidimensional complex. Only a little bit of pseudoscientific chatter kept "Elsewhere" (or "Elsewhen") within the generic confines of *ASF*'s usual fare. Editorial restraints, however, called for a different byline apart from Robert A. Heinlein or Anson MacDonald.

For stories of pure fantasy Campbell published *Unknown* (March 1939 to October 1943; *Unknown Worlds* from October 1941) until the wartime paper shortage caused it to cease after thirty-nine monthly issues. Its fans were the most fanatical of any devoted to reading pulp magazines in the SF/fantasy field and not a few of them, now writers themselves, may be heard still weeping over its demise. *Unknown* was indeed special among the other fantasy magazines, unlike *Weird Tales* (1923–1954) and the rest of them. Campbell's unique formula was to require the author to take one crazy premise per story (some unnatural event or reversal of natural law), then work out its logical implications. No fairy stories, where everything is possible, were permitted.

In fact, this editorial policy differed not in the least from H. G. Wells's famous formula for the writing of science fiction (or what he called the Scientific Romance). In his preface to the collected edition of *The Scientific Romances of H. G. Wells,* he said the trick to writing "fantastic stories" was, "to *domesticate* the impossible hypothesis" by giving it play in the real world of everyday experience, where everything else is homelike and plausible. Suppose a time machine, or some antigravitational device. All other marvels must be excluded. Then the story

becomes human. "How would you feel and what might not happen to you," is the typical question, if for instance pigs could fly and one came rocketing over a hedge at you. How would you feel and what might not happen to you if suddenly you were changed into an ass and couldn't tell anyone about it? [this a classical reference to *The Golden Ass* by Apuleius from about the second century]. Or if you became invisible? No one would think twice about the answer if hedges and houses also began to fly, or if people changed into lions, tigers, cats and dogs, left and right, or if everyone could vanish anyhow.[3]

Wells never violated his own rule, be it with time travel in *The Time Machine* (science fiction) or with the visit from another dimension by an angel in *The Wonderful Visit* (fantasy). This is what Heinlein means when he conflates science fiction and fantasy in his concept of Speculative Fiction. But Wells wrote before the advent of the American genre magazines, in which the whole unified field of romantic literature was minutely subdivided. It was to meet these queer market demands that Heinlein found himself obliged to use different pen names, one for the special-interest readers of each particular genre or subgenre.

By the time he published a third story in *Unknown Worlds* (October 1942), he used the name John Riverside. This was for "The Unpleasant Profession of Jonathan Hoag," and the title says it all—fantasy! Not science fiction, and certainly not a story by Robert A. Heinlein or by Anson MacDonald. To the cognoscenti of the really weird and strange, the title person in bright lights announced a special kind of genre story. Jonathan Hoag is the name of an obscure poet whose works were published by none other than H. P. Lovecraft. As a privately printed book, *The Poetical Works of Jonathan E. Hoag* (1923) was Lovecraft's first appearance in hard covers.[4]

Lovecraft (d. 1937) now has a cultish following of such devotion that prices for his first editions (or more especially, his limited-run pamphlets) are surpassed only by those of Heinlein's in the *Fantasy & Science Fiction* catalogs of L. W. Currey. But Heinlein, in writing his one pen-named story in this tradition, merely glanced upon it by way of showing his mastery over all forms of imaginative literature. After that, he felt free to do another "weird" story under his own name, with "All You Zombies—" in the *Magazine of Fantasy and Science Fiction* (March 1959), a recent and rather more literary magazine whose "and" in the title reflects the influence of Heinlein's unified concept of Speculative Fiction.

By then Heinlein had proved by his commercial success that science fiction could mean whatever he chose it to mean; he no longer had to appeal to the special appetites of the genre market under different disguises. It could mean Robert A. Heinlein, the other science-fiction stories of Anson MacDonald and Lyle Monroe, the near-fantasy of Caleb Saunders, or the weird fantasy of John Riverside. In time, Heinlein had no need to use these other bylines because, by the commanding example of his wide-ranging writings, he had changed the nature of the market and restored imaginative literature to its historic place, as a single romantic field, united within the wider domain of literature proper. For is not all literature imaginative? So Henry James would say.

No doubt this helps to explain why Heinlein signs himself R. A. "Beast" Heinlein in his table of anagrams to *The Number of the Beast* (see Appendix), which novel the author describes as a "romp." Its title refers of course to the Black Beast of Revelations 13, whose "number is six hundred threescore and six." (Biblical allusions abound in Heinlein's work.) The Beast of the Number is taken to signify the almost infinite mansions of the pluriverse and its many rooms of possibility—six to the sixth power to the sixth power. Some of these are explored by the novel's two heroes and two heroines, by means of a "continua craft" guided by a computer named "Gay Deceiver." These include worlds of the fantastic imagination, such as the Mars of Edgar Rice Burroughs, the space-opera settings of E. E. "Doc" Smith, Lilliput, Wonderland (where the four time-space jumpers have tea with Lewis Carroll himself), the Land of Oz, and so on, not to mention story settings from Heinlein's own work. In fact, the novel is a spliced-memory romp through every image dominant in the history of science fiction and fantasy, anticipating by seven years the same technique used by the mainstream novelist Robert Coover in *A Night at the Movies* (1987), in which he splices together in one story all of our outstanding movie memories.

Unlike the dreamy means of purely thought-controlled travel to such unlikely places as in "Elsewhen," the "continua craft" used here is a conventional science-fiction device (conventional after the example set by H. G. Wells's time machine). Even so, it "works by magic, not engineering" (chap. 31), which recalls the mysterious source of energy, derived from another dimension, driving the vehicles of everyday transportation in "Waldo." In the end, all the characters (real and fictional) come together in a kind of science-fiction conference, an "interuniversal Society" celebrating "Multiple-Ego Solipsism." This last phrase is a playful denial of the individual solipsism (the only kind there is in philosophy) for which Heinlein critics (and they, too, appear at this convention) are fond of castigating him; as if his purpose in bidding for a mass audience among youthful readers were to impress them with the easiness of a self-centered philosophy. (The critique of "rugged individualism" once again.) Elsewhere he speaks of "multiperson solipsism" (*Cat*, 359), which is no more irresponsible than the anthropological concept of culture, which says that each separate cultural reality is a collective (or multiperson) project, the shared worldview of each society's conventional making. Or as it is phrased in *Number of the Beast*, "Could anyone ask for plainer statement of the self-evident fact that nothing exists until someone imagines it and thereby gives it being, reality?" (508). Apart from that, " 'solipsism' is a buzz word" (340).

This is the final truth of the matter, in real life as in fiction. The human condition, in its plurality of cultures and multiple worldviews, is not all that different from the worlds created by imaginative writers. Man is one species, but his ways are many, each one of them a profound fiction. That Heinlein knows his anthropology is indubitable, as he shows in *Citizen of the Galaxy*. Here, trader starships the size of metropolitan cities have their own self-contained cultures, whose adaptive purpose is described in one instance by a visiting ethnologist named Margaret Mader (after Margaret Mead, with a touch of whimsy).

For all that, Heinlein is no cultural relativist. He defends his national culture with a realistic sense of patriotism, believing the vision of this nation of nations to be the one best-suited and best-adapted to the cosmic challenges of the human future. Walt Whitman said, "To me, the United States are important because in this colossal drama they are unquestionably designated for the leading parts, for many a century to come. In them history and humanity seem to seek to culminate."[5] For Heinlein, all cultures are equally theatrical, but some are less unreal than others.

With *Number of the Beast* he shows himself completely at home in a playful work of "fantasy comedy or farce," and mixing science fiction fantasy as he pleases. It was not so easily done in the magazines, where the different genres (science fiction the more real, fantasy the less real) he worked were bylined perforce as if by different auctorial voices. Editorial policy called for "other voices, other rooms," to cite the evocative title of the 1948 novel by Truman Capote, which very much deals with the shadow line between reality and dream. Hence the continua craft named Gay Deceiver.

Heinlein did indeed once have his different voices for his different rooms, but now they all shade into one another in the same Heinlein multiverse, with its alternative possibilities—just as in man's actual life on this planet, with its pluriverse of different cultural realities. Now he is free from the old editorial restraints to unite them in a single artistic vision under his one true name. For example, if it was D. D. Harriman who initiated space flight in the Future History stories titled "Requiem" and "The Man Who Sold the Moon" (with a reference to him yet again in "Blowups Happen"), there is also room to accommodate the real thing in the world we know. If it was D. D. Harriman's employee, Captain Leslie LeCroix, who first landed on the moon in this canon, it is no less true that NASA astronauts Neil Armstrong and Colonel Buzz Aldrine also did the same in *Cat* (300). They all share the same honors without contradiction because what they did happened at such a crucial turning point in history, foredestined to come, that any number of ways might have led to the same overdetermined outcome. Thus does Captain LeCroix greet a number of imaginary others, not unlike himself, at the interuniversal convention of multiperson solipsists that concludes *The Number of the Beast*. Not only that. In the same spirit, the Future History hero of "The Long Watch" (*PTT*, 263–76) also appears as a space academy hero in *Space Cadet* (24), one of the juvenile series apart from this other canon.

Yet Heinlein critics find a different unity in his work. They find in "All You Zombies—" the secret that reveals the selfishness of his enduring solipsism. But they overlook the punch line, which goes like this: "*You* aren't really there at all. There isn't anybody but me—." And then, "I miss you dreadfully!" (Solipsism is not so very gratifying, after all.) This is reprinted in the story collection titled, *The Unpleasant Profession of Jonathan Hoag*; the paperback edition is *6 x H: Six Stories by Robert A. Heinlein,* which is advertised, "From sorcery to the fourth dimension." Beneath this headline is the cryptic comment: "These six stories [are] of logical fantasy, of fantastic science." Yet not so cryptic, in light of the author's ultimate purpose. It's all in a day's work for him to play on every possible theme available to fantastic fiction, as a matter of muscular literary exercise. With "All You Zombies—" he simply proves himself able to take up a theme not his own (the solipsist fallacy) and make the definitive statement on it. Why this particular story is always and ever singled out by the critics to reveal his true philosophy is one of the great mysteries of science-fiction criticism.

At all events, the time-space jumpers who make a joyful romp through *The Number of the Beast* give a better clue to his thought. They go everywhere in the author's imagination, crossing from realistic science fiction to dreamlike fantasy. He might well have signed himself the "Gay Deceiver," for his shadowing of these lines of distinction, but he chose to sign himself the "Beast." What is the meaning of this? Remembering that the Beast of Revelations who adopted the number 666 is Lucifer, the brother of the Lord God Jehovah in Milton's retelling of the biblical story, then Heinlein's appellation makes not a little sense. Lucifer means "Light Bringer," under which name Satan works in the service of the divine purpose, whose Creation includes both a nether and an upper region, both equally important to that purpose. So perhaps Heinlein intends to sign himself as the creator of two related fictional worlds, as one who brings equal light to both fantasy and science fiction. Remember also that "666" was the brand name of a healing salve at the time he started writing for *ASF,* during those very same years when its editor viewed his fantasy stories as unfit for the top-of-the-line science-fiction magazine. The number 666 then had on billboards, displayed before the public eye, not a sinister meaning but a benevolent one. Indeed, until the Reformation, this number, called the Mysterium, was displayed on the Pope's mitre.

Thanks now to Heinlein's example, there are no upper and lower regions in the field of science fiction as he has broadly redefined it with the name of Speculative Fiction. He has at last won recognition, by virtue of his own creative success, for the artistic integrity of romantic literature in its dual aspects. That he plays at length on the Miltonic brotherhood of God and Lucifer in *Job: A Comedy of Justice* is perhaps a reflection of this light-bringing triumph. It is, after all, not his first novel to place on the best-seller list of the *New York Times,* where no other science-fiction work (however defined) ever placed before his of 1961, *Stranger in a Strange Land.*

With all this, Heinlein changed the literary landscape in America. The first science-fiction author to break out of the magazine ghetto and its overly specialized genres, he at the same time unified romantic literature on his own terms—now the norm of every writer of Speculative Fiction, his illuminating trade name for it.

Chapter Five
Recognition and Controversy

After World War II Heinlein resumed commercial writing, but now with the ambition "to break out from the limitations and low rates of the pulp science-fiction magazines into anything and everything" (*EU*, 145). This he did along a number of fronts.

His first order of business was to return science fiction to the general circulation magazines where in America it had begun. Having failed to sell his first story of 1939 to *Collier's*, he now made up for lost time by selling a slew of more Future History stories to the "slicks," the *Saturday Evening Post* among them. These helped to win public support for America's growing aerospace industry. In deference to that influence, Walter Cronkite invited Heinlein to speak as guest commentator on CBS-TV during the Apollo 11 mission, which landed two astronauts on the moon, while a third orbited it, on 20 July 1969. Other guests were Arthur C. Clarke (a personal and professional friend), Isaac Asimov (his old colleague at Mustin Field), and Ray Bradbury (not heretofore known as an enthusiast of believable space flight). But these others appeared by virtue of Heinlein's precedent in drawing public attention to the new frontiers of outer space, by his relating them to the homespun simplicity and commonplace human realities of America's old familiar frontiers.

As Heinlein replied to Walter Cronkite's question about the future of space,

I'm not sure how things are going to be done. I'm only certain that they're going to be done in a big way, that we're going out to the planets. That we're going out to the stars. We're going out indefinitely. There's just one equation that everybody knows: $E = EC^2$. It proves the potentiality whereby man can live anywhere there is mass. He doesn't have any other requirement but mass.[1]

It is the same message conveyed to his juvenile readership: "Wherever there is power and mass to manipulate, Man can live" (*RS*, 208). A most complete and convincing example of this principle is dramatized in *Farmer in the Sky,* another of the juveniles, in which the rocky surface of Ganymede (one of the satellites of Jupiter) is easily pulverized by atomic-powered machines into life-giving soil (with the addition of imported bacteria). Here, a new human colony is established with no more effort (no more!) than that required for the colonization of America in the first place, and then the pioneering of the American West. The same breed of men, even young boys and girls, is capable of the same out there in the vasty deeps of unearthly space, with the aid of space-age technology. Updated machines, yes; but the selective human material is of old: brains, hard work, and unconquerable courages.

At this point, Walter Cronkite asked Heinlein about the uplift in American morale "we've all experienced today." Did he think the moon mission would help raise this country's moral spirit? He replied:

I do hope so. There have been too many of the young people who have the defeatist attitude toward things and I hope this will give them the "lift," the "esprit de corps," to realize how terribly important this is. Not alone to them, but to their children, their grandchildren, through thousands of years.[2]

So much again for the so-called "rugged individualism" of Heinlein's frontier ethos. He is nothing if not responsible to the collective human future, as this is advanced (as ever) by its outstanding individualities like D. D. Harriman and other of his capitalist heroes.

Heinlein does indeed hold no brief for monopoly capitalism when it runs out of entrepreneurial steam and goes running to government for shelter from further competition, appealing to that "strange doctrine" used against Dr. Pinero. A good example of his attitude is the animus he directs against a big utility company in "Let There Be Light," collected in 1950, which tells of a small businessman ruined by such politics when he attempts to market a new and cheaper power source of his own invention. But he gets his revenge by releasing the technical details to the press, and the headlines announce, "GENIUS GRANTS GRATIS POWER TO PUBLIC" (in the short story collection, *The Man Who Sold the Moon,* 18). Today, the open secret of superconductivity may have much the same effect on the cheap decentralization of power, hinted at in the Shipstone devices of Heinlein's 1982 novel, *Friday.*

Another thing Heinlein did when he emerged from the magazine ghetto: he is credited with bringing the first modern science-fiction film to the screen, Destination Moon (1950). For this he both drafted the script and served as technical advisor (making sure that the space suits were done right, considering that he had helped to invent them).[3] Each section of the original story is epigraphed with sayings the like of Lazarus Long's, put in the words of one Farquharson, the author of some future *History of Transportation*. He says, for example, looking back as it were on the astronauts killed in the Challenger disaster of 28 January 1986:

If we are to understand these men, we must reorient. Crossing the Atlantic was high adventure—when Columbus did it. So with the early spacemen. The ships they rode in were incredibly makeshift.

They did not know where they were going. Had they known, they would not have gone. (Destination Moon, section 5)

But they did go in Heinlein's history to come. And they will continue to go in the real future, partly owing to his influence. He brought the same inspiring message to the first modern science-fiction television serial, "Tom Corbett, Space Cadet" (1951–1954), based on his juvenile book, *Space Cadet*.[4] This was no dumb "Capt. Video" show; it attracted the attention of many students in my Heinlein course, years before they came to college, motivating their interest in the engineering sciences.

Then there is the fact that Heinlein was the first science-fiction writer to score on the best-seller list of the *New York Times,* starting in 1962 with *Stranger in a Strange Land*. Thereafter he followed up on the same list with *Time Enough for Love* (1973), *The Number of the Beast* (1980), *Friday* (1982), *Job: A Comedy of Justice* (1984), and once again (at age seventy-eight) for eleven weeks with *The Cat Who Walks through Walls* (1985).

Above all, it seems, Heinlein's biggest breakout from the science-fiction ghetto was done with his juvenile series: a set of twelve volumes (1947–1958) published in hard covers by the prestigious house of Scribner's—although each title first appeared as a serial in the science-fiction magazines. (Writing is not like real estate; the same property may be sold to more than one buyer). A thirteenth title, *Starship Troopers* (1959), was not accepted by the series editor, who regarded it as too militaristic for tender juvenile minds. It found a home at Putnam's, however, as an adult novel; but Heinlein continues to regard it as integral to the series he had contracted for with Scribner's. The last of the projected series, *Podkayne of Mars* (1963), was also done by Putnam's, following one of those mistakes every working author tries to avoid—wasting time on a market judged to be unreceptive. Submitted in serial parts to *ASF,* editor John Campbell thought Podkayne or Poddy too precocious to be real, citing his own teenage daughters as the norm. But while Heinlein's exemplary types are unusual, they are not imaginary types; I have seen Poddy more than once among the girl engineering majors in my classroom. In the event, however, it was Heinlein's agent who made the mistake by misreading the author's instructions, which were, send the ms. almost anywhere but to *ASF;* this market is too "sophisticated" for my purpose. After that mixup, at the cost of delayed serialization and a most unwelcome critique from John Campbell, excruciatingly detailed and scolding, Heinlein got a new agent.

The problem with *Starship Troopers* was much more serious. At the same time that Heinlein won wider recognition for science fiction outside the special-interest magazines, he was discovered by the literary critics, whose attention was first drawn by none other than *Starship Troopers;* and they have not ceased kicking at it thirty years later. The fans loved it and gave it a Hugo Award in 1960. But the critics hated it. The fans, by definition, may be counted on to be enthusiastic about almost everything Heinlein writes, but the critics invariably have been unloving. What follows recalls my impressions of the critical literature, without citing particulars from the voluminous bulk, which was uniformly hostile.

The fans have their fanzines, long established, and their own award system—the Hugos, given out at their World Conferences from 1958. Then came the leaguing together of the writers themselves from 1965, through their Science Fiction Writers of America (SFWA). Then followed the academic critics, with their Science Fiction Research Association of 1970 (SFRA).

In 1966 SFWA commenced its annual Nebula Awards, and in 1974 its Grand Masters Nebula Award for Lifetime Achievement, Heinlein receiving its first. SFRA gives what it calls the Pilgrim Award for the best in science-fiction criticism, named after *Pilgrims through Space and Time* by J. O. Baily, a privately printed doctoral dissertation taken by SFRA to be the first work of serious literary criticism in this field.[5] In addition, SFRA issues a regular newsletter and three university-based journals, *Extrapolation* (College of Wooster, Ohio), *Science Fiction Studies* (McGill University, Montreal, published with the financial assistance of the Social Sciences and Humanities Research Council of Canada), and *SF and Fantasy Review* (Florida Atlantic University, Boca Raton, published through the Division of Continuing Education). Here, and elsewhere (including the Sunday *New York Times* book review section) are to be found the anti-Heinlein articles and reviews I allude to when I generalize about Heinlein critics.

SFRA's temper is fairly indicated by its giving of the Pilgrim Award in 1983 to H. Bruce Franklin for his work in 1980 with Oxford University Press, *Robert A. Heinlein: America as Science Fiction,* which turns out to be of more interest to America-hating Marxists than to students of American science fiction. His book marks the height (or depth) of virulent Heinlein foemanship, in which *Starship Troopers* gets especially hard knocks as a fascist work by a fascist author expressing the endemic fascism of his native country. This is the same juvenile title rejected by Scribner's on ideological grounds, even though the house did itself rich by all its previous titles in the series. Thirty years later it was picked up for its "tyrannical views" by Luc Sante, a mainstream critic writing in *Harper's* magazine for October 1985. Tarring Heinlein with that all-purpose smear word, "fascist," it was duly reprinted in the SFRA *Newsletter* for December 1985 (5–21).

What is the meaning of this epithet? At first glance the term *fascist* seems to be a more abusive synonym for tyrannical, as applied to Heinlein's firm belief in noblesse oblige, that is, authority with responsibility, in consideration of the fact that both authority and responsibility are unpopular concepts nowadays (not for Heinlein fans, of course, who are therefore seen in the eyes of the critics to be woefully misguided by a malign mentor). But it is not quite that simple. For Marxists, the fascist label is the meanest one in their vocabulary of anathema, used especially to curse the American idea of national freedom and personal liberty.[6]

Starship Troopers is the story of John Rico, a boy who volunteers for the Terran Federation's Mobile Infantry (M.I.), akin to the U. S. Marine Corps, only with more mobility and fire power. In the course of his training in the M. I., Rico attains manhood; he at last finds purpose in submitting to military discipline and in serving the patriotic cause for which the M. I. was instituted. Patriotism in this case, however, relates to the species patriotism of the whole human community in its planetary dispersion throughout the solar system, united by the government of the Terran Federation, itself a projection of Walt Whitman's nation of nations in fulfilling America's "kosmic" destiny. Its implacable enemies, the "Bugs," are nonhuman aliens of a collectivist nature both in biology and political organization. The job of the M. I. is to defend the Terran frontiers of human freedom against their aggression, modeled after Soviet expansionism. (On that head, they are not unrelated to the "Slugs" who figure in *The Puppet Masters;* at the same time they derive from the socialist Martians of H. G. Wells's *War of the Worlds* [1898]).

The novel opens and closes with battles against the Bugs, surely among the best action scenes ever written in any brand of literature. The bulk of the story, however, is given over to a flashback on Rico's training in the M. I., during which he recalls the teachings of his high school instructor in History and Moral Philosophy, an optional course (like those of today's ROTC programs) taught by an M. I. veteran. He is a viewpoint character who holds, with Heinlein, that military service should be voluntary; conscription amounts to slavery. Only with volunteer recruits can the military count on patriotic self-selection in meeting its highest ideals, those of service, duty, and sacrifice.

The words of Rico's teacher of Moral Philosophy sustain him during the hardships of an infantryman's training: "The noblest fate that man can endure is to place his own material body between his loved home and the war's desolation. . . . This is immutable, true everywhere, throughout all time, for all men and all nations" (74). These words reflect those delivered by Heinlein in his Annapolis address. At that time he said, patriotism "means that you place the welfare of your nation ahead of your own even if it costs you your life."

Here is Heinlein speaking to the novel's praise for "the moral difference . . . between the soldier and the civilian." But it is that same difference, the cultural gap between career officers and liberal-minded intellectuals, that caused the novel to arouse so much hostility among the latter in the first place. For it is only by his dislike of the military that the liberal culture-critic earns his credentials. As James Burnam explains,

The incompatibility between liberalism and the military life, and many of the reasons for it, are obvious and well known. Concepts of equality, nondiscrimination and universal democracy are hard to reconcile with the inequalities, authoritarianism, detailed discrimination and rigid hierarchy that are always and inevitably characteristic of military organization; even if they can be reconciled by some sort of complicated logical exercise, there remains a feeling gap. In his scale of priorities the soldier is professionally committed to place the safety and survival of his country first, and to be ready to sacrifice his life as well as his freedoms and comforts thereto; he must keep the values of social justice and individual rights secondary in rank, if he is to do his soldierly duty; and his devotion to peace, however fervently protested, will always be confused by the fact that his trade is war.[7]

There is, in fact, nothing the Heinlein critic enjoys more than attacking the "military mind" displayed in *Starship Troopers*. How bloody awful of Heinlein still to speak in favor of the professional oath he took in taking up his intended career in the navy.

But there was no objection to *Job*, with its satire on the fundamentalist vision of Heaven, where angelic troops muster the homecoming of all souls after the Last Judgment; and where even here the old military principle of RHIP must prevail—"Rank Hath Its Privileges"—if the quartering of millions and billions of souls in the Heavenly City is to be carried out by their hosts with any angelic efficiency. Denounced by Moral Majority Inc. as an evil work of secular humanism, the critics for once found it safe to stand with the fans.

Yet otherwise, how "fascist" Heinlein's regard for the authoritarian working of military discipline. How "elitist" the Terran Federation's veteranocracy, with its principle of "one veteran, one vote." But here the critics are misled by their favorite animus. Making no impression on them was the fact that 95 percent of the voters in Heinlein's veteranocracy are veterans of the Federation's civil-service bureaucracy. They saw only what they wanted to be negative about, the author's alleged favoring of fascism in the form of a military dictatorship.

This whole line of criticism, sustained against every point of rebuttal ever issued by Heinlein himself (see *EU,* 396–402), finally had its dramatic summary in a satirical science-fiction novel, *Bill the Galactic Hero* (1965) by Harry Harrison. Hailed by the critics as a work of comic genius, it divided Harrison's fellow writers and troubled his fans; both of whom reserved the right to award him his due for later works equally brilliant, but less nervy in touching upon Heinlein's good name. The critics, however, continue to favor this one Harrison title above all, simply because they read it as a digest of everything they despise in *Starship Troopers*. Still, this flap within the science-fiction community, among critics, writers, and fans alike, shows how vital the genre is, in bringing ideological issues to bear on the literary scene; and how important Heinlein is in bringing them to the forefront of attention in American letters generally. If *Starship Troopers* was worth attacking in the pages of *Harper's* magazine in 1985 (how many years after its first publication in 1959?), that is one measure of real recognition—elicited by a worthwhile controversy.

It is, after all, a very ancient and honorable controversy, beginning with the antagonism between Plato and Aristotle. To come right to the point, Heinlein stands with Aristotle, his critics with Plato. Plato the

utopian statist is the patron saint of today's "liberals"—in quotes
because the term once implied, for America's constitutional ancestors in
England, a government liberal in granting its main body of citizens a
generous freedom from state regulation. Now the term implies a large
margin of state control for the public welfare, as if the average citizen
were not to be trusted with looking after his own self-interest—he needs
platonic guardianship.

Aristotle the utopian skeptic is the political ancestor of today's
"conservatives," who take up the position of the traditional liberals,
with whom Heinlein clearly sides. Aristotle is not, however, all that
wild about pure democracy, even as he finds every fault with Plato's
antidemocratic vision of state-run benevolence; "tyranny" was his word
for the end result, "totalitarianism" ours. If democracy then, for all
that, is preferable to statism, how "to insure a responsible electorate"?
That is Heinlein's question (*EU*, 399), as it was for Aristotle. Aristotle
argued that inequalities of native endowment or of acquired traits should
be considered in selection for public office, while disregarding them
altogether when qualifications for plain, nonvoting citizenship are considered.

Heinlein's aversion to a mobocratic misreading of the nation's charter
is what alarms his critics. When he suggests a limitation of the franchise
to veterans of the Terran Federal service; when he says that anybody
civic-minded enough to serve the Federation in any capacity, military
or civil, is better qualified to vote than are its passive citizens; when
thereby he makes the general point that the right to vote should be
earned in some way—that his critics take for antidemocratic heresy. In
blaming him for that with such ideological ire, as if Aristotle and others
had not long preceded him, they surely give him far more credit than
he deserves.

As Heinlein pointed out to his interviewer from the *Wall Street
Journal* in 1985, "most of the criticism I've seen is an admission by
the critic of his political alignment rather than an understanding of my
work." Heinlein sees his critics taking him to task because they imagine
him to be a rival statist when in fact he is no statist at all. The critics,
in other words, claim a monopoly on social and political thought, and
anybody who has something to say on the governing of men, outside
the purview of righteous Platonism, is by definition a fascist.

Thus do the critics ignore the fact that the political message of
Starship Troopers is no more than a playful variation on a kind of
science-fiction story done by Mark Twain, as Heinlein patiently explains

(*EU*, 399). He compares his work to that of Twain's "Curious Republic of Gondour" (1875), leaving it up to the reader to verify this parallel for himself. But that will not be easy because the Twain story remains no less heretical now than it was in its own day, and it is not to be found in any of the "complete" stories of Mark Twain currently on the market. "The Curious Republic of Gondour" is curious for its electoral rules. These have it that "every citizen, however poor or ignorant, possessed one vote, so universal suffrage still reigned; but if a man possessed a good common-school education and no money, he had two votes," and so on by degrees; the more education the more votes, until the more-schooled had it in their power to outvote the uneducated rich concerned only with pelf. But while this is a blow at the parvenue rich of the "gilded age" (one of Twain's favorite targets), it no less deprives the uneducated masses of carrying their numerical weight.

It was Emerson who said, "Majorities, the argument of fools!" Twain echoed this in the words of Huck Finn who said, "The fools . . . ain't that a big enough majority in any town?"[8] Lazarus Long says the same: "Does history record *any* case in which the majority was right?" (*LL*, 347). And so did Walt Whitman, the epic poet of American democracy, when he warned of "the appaling dangers of universal suffrage."[9]

It's an old theme in American literature, this tension between democratic ideals and political reality. In fact, it was a question fastened upon by our very first novelist, Hugh Henry Brackenridge, who showed himself to be an aristocratic democrat when he wrote the following in his *Modern Chivalry* (1819):

A democracy is beyond question the freest government; because under this, every man is equally protected by the laws, and has equally a voice in making them. But I do not say an equal voice; because some men have stronger lungs than others, and can express more forcibly their opinions of public affairs. Others, though they may not speak very loud, yet have a faculty of saying more in a short time; and even in the case of others, who speak little or none at all, yet what they do say containing good sense, comes with greater weight; so that all things considered, every citizen, has not, in this sense of the word, an equal voice. But the right being equal, what harm if it is unequally exercised?[10]

If Heinlein writes to this same point, he maintains the honorable tradition of New World chivalry, which his critics condemn as "elitist."

Walt Whitman rejects such condemnation. Nowhere but in America, he said, were the ideals of European chivalry truly realized; only the American version of it "comes under the words, *Noblesse Oblige,* even for a national rule or motto."[11] In other words, it is only the American official at his best, representative of his people and responsible to them, who dares lay claim to this ancient motto, "rank imposes obligations."

This is the modern chivalry that animates Heinlein's veteranocracy, a true echo of the nation's Puritan heritage, founded on the political thought of John Calvin, who held "the best defense against tyranny to lie in a form of government in which aristocracy (the rule of the best) is mingled with democracy."[12] In *Starship Troopers* those who have earned the right to vote include not only the soldiers of the M. I. but all those many others who trouble themselves with civic duties. Who are these people, then, if not President Thomas Jefferson's "natural aristocracy"? They merely adhere to the nation's founding ideals.

On one point Heinlein agrees with his critics who charge that *Starship Troopers* glorified the military. "I hope I accomplished that," he said to his interviewer from the *San Francisco Examiner* in 1986. "The poor bloody mudfoot, the infantryman who for centuries put his frail body on the line for home, loved ones—and for the critics who often outlive him—needs some glorifying. That's the least I can do" (see also *EU,* 398).

Heinlein is not ashamed of his first calling, the trade of war, a most noble and necessary profession, denied him only by ill health. Yet he knows, from his own disappointed ambition, that any nation has need of such men as he in its armed forces. All the better for America that such men are self-selected for duty and sacrifice; patriotism cannot be conscripted. So what if the civilian populace does not appreciate them, and what may happen if it doesn't? His answer: the U. S. A. "has a system free enough to let its heroes work at their trade. It should last a long time—unless its looseness be destroyed from inside" (*Glory Road,* 262).

Chapter Six
Sex and Culture Criticism

The next big turning point in Heinlein's wider recognition was the controversy lavished on *Stranger in a Strange Land* (1961), which won a Hugo Award the year of its publication, as did *Starship Troopers* (1959) a year after. As already mentioned, *Stranger* was the first science-fiction novel to place on the national best-seller list published weekly by the Sunday *New York Times*. It was also the first work of that genre to deal openly with sex. Are these two firsts related? Heinlein critics like to think so, as if sex were some prurient whim the author indulged the better to exploit the market and catch its undeserving attention.

But the history of the American novel, quite apart from the personal predilections of its authors, records a real change in society's operating code of acceptable sexual behavior, and this shift in moral weather is duly registered in what the fiction market will accept. One literary historian of this change observes, "The indexes of sexuality will read all the way from the extraordinary innocence of Howells' society, through the self-conscious sinning of Dreiser's characters, to the casual promiscuity of Kerouac's beatniks."[1] When Heinlein began writing in *ASF*, mainstream literature was at the Dreiser stage, while the editorial policy of the romantic underground (aimed mainly at juvenile readers) remained located at the stage of Howellsian primness.

Ironically it was Dreiser himself who upheld these older standards in that industry. The while he was forming his own literary career, he served as editor for Street and Smith Publications, then the biggest chain of pulp magazines in the business, with *ASF* one of its titles. Moreover, his first stories appeared in the pulps. Indeed, even after he established himself in the highbrow market (only to change it in his radical way by 1900 with *Sister Carrie*), he was not above publishing in *Ghost Stories* as late as 1929. Nor was Dreiser the only modern American author to begin in the innocent genres of the pulp trade. Upton Sinclair first wrote for *West Point Stories*. Ring Lardner, who started out as a sports columnist, did his first fiction for *Baseball Stories*.

Before Tennessee Williams won fame as a playwright, he wrote short stories for *Weird Tales*.[2]

With *Stranger in a Strange Land* Heinlein jumped from the Howells to the Kerouac stage, causing his critics renewed dismay. In this case they are the SFRA critics alone, academics with a special interest in science fiction as a branch of popular culture. Their complaint is that *Stranger* is a failed novel because science fiction and sex don't mix. This amounts to advising the author: please to keep science fiction in immature magazines where it belongs. The irony of this critical position (not shared by the science-fiction writers, who know a good selling point when they see one) is hard to overlook. Given that the mission of the SFRA academics is to raise science fiction up and out of its magazine ghetto and give it critical respectability, they are remarkably timid about claiming mature privileges for the lowly genre they purport to wish to elevate. SFRA has proud links with the Popular Culture Association; but in the end this results in a regressive wish to preserve the genre's chastity intact, like a museum artifact, by way of reserving to the SFRA a privileged field of enlightened nostalgia.

The upshot of that critical policy is to prevent Heinlein's emergence from the pulps (like Dreiser's and others') to rank among the great writers of American literature. His own reply to these patronizing and contemptuous critics is shrewdly to the point, "I had to wait for the mores of America to change. I saw them changing, and my timing was right."

All the same, the novel's dealing is promiscuity fails to fit the mainstream's carnal attitude toward sex. The modernist pretense that reproduction is only an adjunct of sex, something not in the nature of the act itself, is not his. He is far from being that dishonest. Sex is for making babies, yet another "conservative" stance that annoys his "liberal" critics. This is implicit in a saying of Lazarus Long, with regard to the proper function of the military: "All societies are based on rules to protect pregnant women and young children" (*LL*, 242). Besides, not in *Stranger in a Strange Land*, nor in any other adult title, does Heinlein ever graphically depict sexual behavior. Never pornographic, yet he is called "sexist" by nearly every critic in the business. His military credo, you see (the one voiced at his Annapolis lecture), is based on that rule of distressed ships at sea: "Women and children first." Males are expendable; child-bearing females and their young are not. If Heinlein were attacked on this point of traditional morality and given wider recognition in consequence of such a controversy, he might well take it as a mark of honor. He is ever the officer and a gentleman.

The protagonist of *Stranger in a Strange Land* (whose working title was *The Man from Mars*) is Valentine Michael Smith.[3] Like Rudyard Kipling's Mowgli, the man from Mars named Smith was reared from infancy by nonhumans, in this case Martians. But his home world is not the Mars of the Mariner IX orbital surveys (1971–72) nor that of the Viking Lander (1976). It is rather more like the Mars of Edgar Rice Burroughs (its canals now polluted, its aery cities abandoned under the impress of Terran colonists), as derived from the false astronomy of Percival Lowell.[4] But never mind. Heinlein's Martians (here and in the juvenile *Red Planet*) belong to science fiction no less than do the Selenites of *The First Men in the Moon* (1901) by H. G. Wells, whose comments on human affairs from the distant vantage point of that cosmic platform have not in the least been subverted by the landing of NASA astronauts upon the lunar surface in 1969. So, too, with Heinlein. He is not to be discounted for his fantastic Mars. (The passing of its pristine glories is lamented by the blind poet of the spaceways in "The Green Hills of Earth.")

Learning the secrets of hypnotism and magic from his Martian upbringers, Smith is a young adult by the time he is rescued and brought home to the planet of his natural parents (early explorers mysteriously lost). Here on earth he is tutored in American ways by a famous businessman-writer and huckster named Jubal Harshaw, who advises him how to make commercial use of his powers by setting up a profitable religious cult. The advice is well founded, on the premise that the best way to get rich in America (if not only in California), is to start a new religion.

There is a measure of truth in this, as evidenced by the Church of Scientology founded by L. Ron Hubbard (a former *ASF* writer), whose obituary in the *New York Times* for 28 January 1986 was front-page news. Mark Twain held the same cynical view on the success of Mary Baker Eddy and her First Church of Christ, Scientist. It was his pet peeve, and critics complained he gave it too much attention.

Heinlein, probably, would not agree. For he, too, long has been concerned with social forces in America making for such cults. One of his prewar *ASF* stories, "If This Goes On—," is about the same kind of cultish fervor elevated to the power of a theocratic dictatorship, voted in by the masses after a wave of popular enthusiasm for the Reverend Nehemiah Scudder, its "First Prophet." The evils of universal suffrage, of which Twain warned, here bear fruit when Scudder is elected president of the United States, only to destroy its Constitution. For all the charges of right-wing extremism leveled against Heinlein, he remains deeply suspicious of today's Moral Majority, Inc. (founded 1980), with its mixture of conservative politics and biblical fundamentalism. That its preachers are potential Nehemiah Scudders are to him a fearful prospect. The measure of that, in "If This Goes On—," may be tested against the Iranian Revolution, with its fundamentalist Muslim clerics raising the Ayatollah Khomeni to theocratic power.

So it is not very likely that Valentine Smith's water-sharing cult brought from Mars, where on his arid home planet it had some practical use in making for political unity, is taken by Heinlein as a serious model for the fixing of human brotherhood on Terra, awash with oceanic waters as Mars is not. Valentine for love, Smith for commonality: his name spells out the idea of universal amity. But his cult presupposes the ability of humans to learn Martian ways, above all the skill "to Grok" each other once instructed in this telepathic technique, as it seems to be. Sincere communicants of this cult are expected, in hippie language, "to dig" each other, to be able to communicate with a perfect mutual understanding beyond words. Once this relaxed sense of fellow feeling is mastered in each little hedonistic "nest" of naked polygamous joy, the devout are then prepared "to Grok" the rest of the universe as well. Standing apart from the materialist concerns of a love-barren world, they show by the force of their example the way to salvation. Heretics who get in the way of this mission are "discorporated" by Martian magic.

In the event, the novel became a how-to-do-it cult book among successors to Kerouac's beatniks, the hippies. In the Haight-Ashbury district of San Francisco and elsewhere these dope-taking dropouts of the so-called counterculture formed "nests" of free sexual sharing and group nudity. They did this, as they were wont to say, "by the book" out of Heinlein's book—much to the author's surprise. They were not his hippies, as were the beatniks the road companions of Jack Kerouac, whose "beat" style of life he himself enjoyed and described in *On the Road* (1957) and *The Dharma Bums* (1958).

Heinlein critics, however, were wont to take this outcome as the intended purpose of the author, thus granting him great magical powers indeed. But the cult he describes is a generic one, far from his own devilish invention, a type given to the principle of "agapemone," the very name of a disreputable association of men and women living promiscuously on a common fund in Somersetshire in late nineteenth-century England. Its failed utopian promise is a sad story, played out once again in the nesting habits of Valentine Smith and his idealistic followers. (There was that little problem of unwanted children.)

Yet the critics took *Stranger* to be a promotion of the type of agapemone cult Heinlein himself has the gravest doubts about, even to the point of satirizing it. But hints of that in the book were overlooked most readily by those eternal patrons of youth culture, who actually rejoiced in what they saw as its countercultural directives. On the negative side, the recent *Harper's* article attacking Heinlein is the meanest, blaming him for being "a major influence on Charles Manson."[5]

The allusion here is to a psychotic madman with a criminal record who, the most hateful of Heinlein's critics are wont to say with some glee, took up *Stranger* as his bible of the one true religion. As it turns out, this is a complete fabrication. According to *Time* magazine, a few weeks after Manson's indictment for murder, his lawyer "discovered that he may have murdered by the book"—Heinlein's book. Given that revelatory text, so the story goes, Manson founded his own "nest," the Manson Family, comprising five dependent and servile female followers, living in disrepute at a deserted movie-location ranch in California. He is said to have named his first illegitimate child Valentine Michael Smith, and nicknamed his parole officer Jubal. But lacking Martian magic, so the falsified story continues, his Family did its job of "discorporating" actress Sharon Tate, and six other people, in her Hollywood home, with plain ordinary butcher knives.[6]

Heinlein looked into this story (it first broke in what he calls "a yellow journalistic piece in the San Francisco *Chronicle*"), with a view to mounting a libel suit against the original concocter of these malicious lies. For his own lawyer had discovered, by interviewing Manson in jail, that the murderer had never read *Stranger,* had never even heard of its author's name. Indeed, he turned out to be scarcely literate, a reader of no books at all. (But the original article was unsigned, so no suit could be mounted.)

Mark Twain said, in reference to agapemone types, "naked people have little or no influence in society."[7] But Heinlein critics, who favor them when it suits, do. So now it is gospel in the critical literature that Heinlein is at fault for the Manson murders. It is justifiably a sore point with him.

To be sure, Valentine Smith is the proverbial Martian, viewing American society from the outside, his cosmic detachment standing for an idealistic viewpoint. He thereby defamiliarizes our accustomed affairs, making them look strange and stupid, worthy of indictment and fit for radical reform. This is an old tradition in Western literature, going back to Montesquieu's *Persian Letters* of 1721, a work of culture criticism contributing to the philosophy of the French Revolution. But note that Heinlein's "Persian," now Martian, is not the one who makes the critique in question. It is made by Jubal Harshaw (a Heinlein viewpoint character); in a switch on the old tradition, it is he who instructs the man from Mars in his Martian detachment, down to the last knowing detail of his learned estrangement. Smith's utopian ideals, then, are derived indirectly from Harshaw, who elicits them point for point against his lessons in culture criticism. The implication is, whatever is wrong with American reality cannot be rectified by Smith's cult of agapemone. The impossible powers and freedoms he preaches only call attention, by contrast, to wrongs that are to be righted by practical reforms, arising from that enhanced sense of American self-awareness that it is the novel's true purpose to induce, in keeping with what is basically good about America.

Stranger is a strong-minded work of culture criticism, no doubt about it. One of the midshipmen at Annapolis, in the question-and-answer session following Heinlein's lecture there, asked to know if this novel did not contradict the patriotic oratory he had just listened to. Heinlein's answer was a simple "no." This young warrior in the service of his country had yet to learn that the questioning of America is not un-American; that, rather, it is at the very core of what it means to be a patriotic American, distinguishing ours from all other traditions of national loyalty. We alone accept critical self-reflection as the essential part of our New World identity, our different "moral identity" as Walt Whitman put it, himself demonstrating it in the contrast between his poetical celebration of American democracy and his very hard-nosed skeptical prose on American failings and shortcomings. It is for this virtue, Mark Twain said, no greater power than ours "has arisen upon this the only soil in this world that is truly sacred to liberty."[8]

In chapter 13 of *A Connecticut Yankee* Twain sums up his views on how American patriotism differs from that of Europe's outworn medieval loyalties:

My kind of loyalty was loyalty to one's country, not to its institutions or its office-holders. The country is the real thing . . . to watch over. . . . Institutions are extraneous, they are its mere clothing, and clothing can wear

out . . . become ragged. . . . To be loyal to rags . . . that is a loyalty of
unreason, it is pure animal; it belongs to monarchy, was invented by monarchy.
. . . The citizen who thinks he sees that the commonwealth's political clothes
are worn out, and yet holds his peace, and does not agitate for a new suit
is disloyal; he is a traitor. That he may be the only one who thinks he sees
this decay, does not excuse him; it is his duty to agitate anyway.

The author of *Stranger,* his most-favored adult work to date, talks very
like that Connecticut Yankee. Besides, he says, if there is anything like
"a universal best seller" among his works in all countries where it has
been translated, it is *Stranger.* Although the novel is not credited for
its refined subtlety, certainly its range of opinions on things aesthetic,
moral, political, economic, or whatever, is the most complete and compact
consistent with orderly storytelling. It is for his punchy judgments and
opinions on such matters, as well as for the unfailing drive and wit of
the narrative line itself, that Heinlein fans read him with more appre-
ciation than do his humorless critics. The majority of fans, witless hippies
aside, sense what Heinlein is doing in his Twain-like watch over their
country, as he takes its institutions to task when they make rags of its
ideals.

How odd it is, then, to find the same critics (those academics who
do rightfully act as custodians of our literary heritage) quoting Twain
in defense of their preoccupation with America's fallibility and limits.
For this, Twain is regarded not only as our first great national author,
but as the first to set the modern temper in American literature. It
was Lionel Trilling, in the Preface to his *Beyond Culture* (1965), who
said, that "modern" writing is characterized chiefly by "the adversary
intention, the actually subversive intention." Its "clear purpose," he
said, is that "of detaching the reader from the habits of thought and
feeling that the culture imposes, of giving him a ground and vantage
point from which to judge and condemn, and perhaps revise, the culture
that produced him."

By that measure, Twain is not a modern writer; and neither is
Heinlein. Both of them have more yeas than nays to say to the culture
that produced them. More to revise than condemn is their aim in both
cases. No more than Twain, Heinlein is no destructive critic, neither
subversive, adversative, or "modern."

Jubal Harshaw's instruction of Smith in the particulars of culture
criticism is not what it seems to be; it is not actually keyed to the
captious tune of Thrilling's nay-saying modernism. Harshaw speaks

harshly, to be sure; he appears the spokesman for the worst in American culture as Heinlein himself judges it. Indeed, Harshaw's crass talk about exploiting the market for his hack writings, and then for Valentine Smith's cult under his guidance, is right out of H. L. Mencken's most celebrated essay, "On Being an American" (in *Prejudices: Third Series,* 1922), in which he cynically lays out the simple rules for snaring that bird of no season, the *"boobus Americanus."* But it needs to be made clear that Mencken's free-wheeling invective against American institutions is directed from a conservative position. So is Jubal Harshaw's. That is why he figures as a Heinlein viewpoint character, no different in temper from The Admiral who addressed the Naval Academy in 1973, twelve years after the publication of *Stranger.* At bottom he speaks the language of Carlyle's "eternal yea," a phrase actually appearing in the novel (65, chap. 8).

Like Whitman, Twain, and Mencken before him, Heinlein has the confidence to assert the fundamental values of American culture, for all of its failings, on the unabashed premise of its basic superiority. It takes moral courage to uphold that position in these days of cultural relativism, when a preoccupation with American shortcomings is taken for the moral high ground, in a virtuous display of faultfinding that levels down this nation of nations to the ranks of the unspecial others.

In foreign affairs Heinlein's position means that the national spirit of the U. S. is basically right in its contest with the party spirit of the U. S. S. R.; democracy is morally better than a one-party dictatorship, whose expansionist policy is basically wrong. Thus the conflict between us is basically their fault. It is a cosmic projection of that enemy the M. I. fights in *Starship Troopers,* and a board game based on and named after it has for a subtitle, *Man vs. Monster.*[9] The collectivist imperium of the Bugs out there is the Evil Empire of the twenty-second century.

In domestic affairs Heinlein defends America's dominant middle-class morality against another kind of relativism, one that equates all sub-cultures as merely alternative life-styles, equally adequate to fulfill the national promise; as if Americanization were no longer the best way for minority groups to solve their problems. But when Heinlein asserted the values of a national norm, with special reference to a black underclass in *Farnham's Freehold* (1964), the critics branded him "racist."

When *Farnham's Freehold* appeared, at the height of the Black Power movement, it met with a storm of critical indignation. The title hero is flung into a future in which the rule of North America has passed to the Black Muslims. (Never mind how Farnham gets there; time travel is a convention in science fiction that needs no more explaining than Athena's guidance of spear throwing in Homer). As in "If This Goes On—," yet another fundamentalist sect has come to power, and with the same disagreeable results. At the same time Heinlein dramatizes Mark Twain's prophecy of 1885 that within a hundred years the formerly enslaved blacks of America would turn things around and "put whites under foot."[10] Or at least they might be disposed to do so, if emancipation were not completed with the elimination of racial prejudice. The unlovely victory of black culture in Heinlein's novel is nothing if not a testimony to Twain's enlightened plea for racial and cultural pluralism; yet for all that, a pluralism harmonized with the majority values of the nation's founders.

This patriotic note was another sore point with the critics. They jabbed at the novel's hero, Hugh Farnham, for the single-minded attention he gave to rescuing his family from black enslavement, and then for defending the family freehold upon the return of the Farnhams to the postwar anarchy of the "present" time. As it happens, the whole family had been thrown into the future by the mysterious effects of an atomic bomb blast, while hiding in their fallout shelter during World War III. Somehow getting back to their own time, in the midst of wartorn chaos, they establish their own freehold and fly the American flag over it. The critics found this offensive, for what appeared to them to be no more than pure selfishness united with racism, the whole miserable scene falsely wrapped in bunting.

But Hugh Farnham, in restoring his family to the best security he can manage, does nothing out of keeping with sound Christian doctrine. St. Paul says: "But if any does not take care of his own, and especially of his household, he has denied the faith and is worse than an unbeliever" (Timothy I, 5:8). The faithful are of course obliged to be helpful to others, loving one's neighbor as oneself, etc. But as the Bishop of Hippo (St. Augustine) observed, while the Roman Empire fell into anarchy all about his diocese in Tunisia, the religious person's "first duty is to look out for his own home, for both by natural and human law he has easier and readier access to their requirements" (*City of God*, chap. 14).

Yet when Heinlein defends the traditional ethics of Christian civilization, it is not seen in him; it is "rugged individualism" all over again, and worse. Moreover, Hugh Farnham frees himself and his family on the same principles that guide black emancipation in *The Narrative of the Life of Frederick Douglass: An American Slave* (1845). Its famous words, "No slave is ever freed, *save he free himself,*" are those quoted by Heinlein elsewhere, without attribution, in "Logic of Empire" (*PTT,* 401). He clearly expects the reader to recognize the source, this great classic of Afro-American Literature.

In truth, there is nothing in Heinlein's work that goes against the idealistic words of President Ronald Reagan, spoken on the night of 4 July 1986, when the Statue of Liberty was rededicated:

And tonight, we reaffirm that, Jew and Gentile, we are one Nation under God; that black and white, we are one nation indivisible; that Republican and Democrat, we are all Americans.

That is the patriotism The Admiral, as ever, is ready to serve, in the hope that things will never come to ruin as they did for Hugh Farnham's America. Indeed, the Howard Families (in *Methuselah's Children*) comprise Americans of all races and ethnic backgrounds.

But when the fans themselves complain about anything done by Heinlein, that is time to pay attention. They didn't much like his mammoth novel of 1970, *I Will Fear No Evil,* his biggest book to that date. Their lament is: too much sex. On the face of it, this complaint is unexpected; they didn't object to the same in *Stranger.* Even so, this other sold fairly well among them, as it did to readers outside the science-fiction community. Those inside it, however, were attracted only by what they called its "good parts," which were not the sexual parts.

I Will Fear No Evil is the story of a very rich old man, a capitalist of D. D. Harriman's prowess, whose body fails him though his mind is quick as ever. His only hope, to carry forward his destiny-making enterprises, is a new body. A new body is found, just in time before he expires. It turns out to be that of a nubile young lady, his highly intelligent and sexy black secretary. Her body is ready at the right moment, she the victim of those hazardous times of the near future in North America, when a few "safe" zones of well-lighted plush are surrounded by "abandoned areas" of barbarian darkness and danger; and where constant alertness against those on the "outside" beating on the doors of the "inside" is the rule.

These were the "good parts," according to the fans; these few glimpses of a future world based on today's grim trends. Heinlein disavows being the anticipator of things to come that H. G. Wells was, yet his fans tend to read him as a social prophet in the Wellsian tradition, remembering as they do his early Future History stories. They are perhaps encouraged by the allusion in "The Roads Must Roll" to Wells's *Anticipations* of 1901 (*PTT*, 42). But the term "Future History" is not Heinlein's; it was coined by his magazine editor, John Campbell, as a selling point. It was Campbell who introduced the whole series under the heading, "History to Come," in his *ASF* editorial for May 1941 (p. 5f.). Everybody likes to believe in the magic of crystal balls; but Heinlein himself never claimed to be oracular. He says in a postscript to *Revolt in 2100*, a collection of such stories, they "were never meant to be a definitive history of the future (concerning which I know no more than you do)" (189).

The rest of the book the fans rather endured as a duty to read, taking little pleasure in it. The bulk of the story is told in a long dialogue between the old man's brain (his name is Johann) and the residual mind of his new female body (her name is Joan), from whom Johann learns more about sexuality than he ever thought possible to know or feel. Familiar with the fallacies of dual consciousness, out of their habitual scorn for the worst kind of cheap Sci Fi flicks and their dumbo stories of brain transplants, the fans were not fooled; they know that old brain plus new body still adds up to only one mind. Mind goes with brain, and it is not possible for another one to reside in the brainless donor body. Yet Heinlein gives them an out, in suggesting that the dual consciousness of Johann and Joan is but the former's delusion.

At the same time, Heinlein did not expect his newly found general readership to be so fastidious. Its generous response was to delight in all the kinky possibilities of the book's initial premise. For example, Johann/Joan getting himself/herself impregnated by the old man's lawyer, adding yet a third level of consciousness, as they all debate how their offspring will carry on whatever it is that Johann wanted carried on, in this newborn carrier of unusually combined capacities.

There is more kinky fun, as Johann gets used to his female body, with the help of Joan's tough-minded advice. Every problem of the most practical sort is played out to the last trifling degree. The initial premise, utterly fantastic, is domesticated by swamping it in a morass of commonplace minutiae. But that's the whole point, of course, in the most sustained joke in the history of fantastic fiction. It derives from the technique of making the weird seem plausible, as practiced in the pages of *Unknown Worlds*, where the impossible (a brain transplant in this case) is made the basis for working out its logical consequences. In milking this convention with the laborious thoroughness of Euclid's textbook of geometry, Heinlein cannot be faulted for lack of imagination in figuring every angle. But the critics faulted him for the lengths he took it, and the fans didn't get the joke at all.

For once the fans are in agreement with the critics, even if for different reasons. So unusual is this case, that it may signal a serious lapse on Heinlein's part. But this is far from certain; the author's prose is as vigorous and high-spirited as ever. Only one thing is clear: the critics are mistaken when they say he is "too explicit," even "sexist" for his vulgar exploitation of a like-minded market. The worst that can be said is that he is too giggly. There is indeed a lot of kidding and bantering about sex and its various taboo-breaking variations, all in the name of personal freedom; but the novel lacks any descriptions of the act itself in any form. The only graphic depiction of sex by Heinlein occurs in *Farnham's Freehold,* but significantly this deals with the reproductive end of it, in a very gutsy scene showing Hugh Farnham delivering his daughter's child, as if to say: that's what sex is all about. But in *Fear No Evil* Heinlein's treatment of sex and the body remains well within the range of Walt Whitman's "religion of healthy mind-edness."[11] Sex is for having babies and for cementing love and family, in the course of reproducing the ongoing life of the species.

As Lazarus Long says, "There can be sex without love, and love without sex," but love itself is "a spiritual quality rather than a physical one" (*TEL,* 124, 132). This from the oldest dirty old man in the universe (1912–4272).

But for all that, his "amorous manias" (dare one quote Fourier?) are the final test of sexual morality. If Johann/Joan has his/her special baby in a most exotic way, it still is the human process that counts, at both the species level and the personal level of married love and intimacy.

One way to look at Johann and Joan is to see them as a married couple, whose intimacy is carried to the ultimate of sex equality. This ideological theme is easy to overlook, now it is fairly well taken for the enlightened norm, thanks to the better efforts of the woman's movement. Heinlein's view on this is no longer radical, as it was when he began in the asexual pulps, where he perforce had to express it less directly.

What a remarkable thing it is to find in "The Unpleasant Profession of Jonathan Hoag," that most Lovecraftian and "escapist" of fantasy stories, a realistic portrait of the companionate marriage, which it is the story's hidden purpose to celebrate. Against the weirdest threats possible to imagine raised against them, a husband and wife hold together not only in mutual love but in friendship. All around them the world and its people is not what it seems, a ghastly setting recalling the lines of Poe's "Conqueror Worm,"

> Mere puppets they, who come and go
> At bidding of vast formless things
> That shift the scenery to and fro.

(Not so farfetched, this tale can be matched by the real-life horror story told by Elena Bonner in *Alone Together* [1986], about her exile with husband Andrei D. Sakharov in Gorky, where every act of everyday life is converted by the stage-managing Soviet authorities into a bitter struggle.) A similar couple go to their heavenly reward for upholding the same ideals of sex quality in yet another fantasy story. "The Man Who Travelled in Elephants," reprinted in a collection titled *6 x H*.

Or again, Heinlein has not overlooked comradeship between the sexes among fellow professionals in the workplace, as with the research team of Doctors Archie Douglass and Mary Lou Martin, both young physicists in "Let There be Light," one of the earliest of the Future History stories. Their collaboration in the development of the Douglass-Martin sunpower screens basic to the coming energy revolution (see Future History chart under "Technical Data," *PTT*, 660) is a learning experience in human relations for Archie, who began the relationship with all the usual male prejudices of the time. In overcoming them (finally to marry his partner Mary Lou), Archie undergoes a progressive change of the sort to be found nowhere in the mainstream literature of the time. But here it is, in the May 1940 issue of *Super Science Stories*. Perhaps only in the disguise of fantasy or super science was Heinlein able to exemplify the virtues of his own marriage, a model of loving companionship, and to uphold this radical ideal against the patriarchal model dominant in those days. The same thing carries forward in the eqalitarian marriage of Alex and Margrethe extolled in the recent novel, *Job* (1984). Indeed, Heinlein takes it as a natural fact of life that women excel men in so many important ways, that he is quite prepared to foresee the future recognition of this fact in a change of language habits, with *her* replacing *him* as a general term "when both masculine and feminine are implied" (*TEL*, 146).

At all events, after *Fear No Evil* came the even bigger and more important novel, *Time Enough for Love* (1973), which is given a separate place (out of sequence) in the subsequent chapter. It very nearly was Heinlein's last work, and for that reason alone it deserves being set apart for special treatment. Had he closed out his career with this, it would have been a monumental end. But fortunately there was more *(Number of the Beast, Friday, Job, Cat Who Walks through Walls),* and there is at least one more title yet to come, as he schedules his next novel (as of this writing) for publication on his eightieth birthday, 7 July 1987. (Probably his last work, it is indexed in his files as opus 189).

After proofreading the galleys of *Time Enough for Love,* he and his wife spent 1976 and 1977 on blood drives all over the country, recruiting thousands of new blood donors. For a man who treasures his family privacy, he could not resist going public for this good cause. To Heinlein, a well-stocked blood bank is one of the essentials of modern civilization, in order to provide adequate stocks for even the rarest blood types known to medical science. Himself a member of the Rare Blood (donors) Club, he did an article for the 1976 edition of the *Compton Yearbook* on the history of hematology, released in pamphlet form under the title, *Are You a "Rare Blood"?* For the 1975 edition he wrote on the latest developments in theoretical physics (reprinted in *EU,* 472–93), which only goes to show that the science in his "hardcore" science fiction is not fantastic, even as his fantasy is based on the hard realities of the human condition. (The *Compton Yearbook* is a publication of Encyclopedia Britannica, Inc.)

Following that outburst of civic activity, he was half paralyzed by the onset of a TIA—the medical acronym for a transient ischemic attack (not a stroke, but the prelude to one). The cause was blockage of the left internal carotid artery on the left side of his brain. The possible cure, carotid bypass surgery, then was a state-of-the-art operation dependent on the latest experimental applications of medical technology derived from the nation's space program. The performance of this operation on a man over seventy years old was not only medical news, it was political news. After his recovery Heinlein was called upon, on 19 July 1979, to testify before the House Select Committee on Aging, and before the House Committee on Science and Technology on the subject of the Applications for Space Technology for the Elderly and Handicapped (see *EU,* 500–13). Curiously enough, Mark Twain before him had been called to a like hearing, in 1886, to testify on the nation's copyright laws.

Heinlein then returned to print with *Number of the Beast* (1980), full of in-jokes and anagrams for the delight of his fans. It was his way of saying "hello again" after a return to life. Never one to write puzzle books à la James Joyce, he made this one different. His fans recognized the fact, and went on straightaway to decode it. His answers, published for the first time, are given in the Appendix. But non-fans enjoyed the book as well. A good storyteller has no one special audience, and the book was another best-seller.

After that came *Friday* (1982), whose heroine is named after the Norse fertility goddess Freya. Indeed, she herself is one of those mythical creatures of science-fiction convention, a bionic construct, partly human and partly artificial. This gives her the advantage of an outsider's viewpoint, like that of the proverbial Martian, which she does not hesitate to articulate. She delivers Heinlein's up-to-date judgments in his usual posture as culture critic.

In this case (again a story about a near-future Earth, as in *Fear No Evil*), he spots a number of unhealthy trends leading on to the decline of terrestrial civilization. North America is balkanized into dozens of little sovereignties (such as the Chicago Imperium, the California Confederacy, and the Mexican Revolutionary Kingdom) within a global polity degenerated into some four hundred "territorial states." Is this a fantastic prophecy? Not in the least. Right now in the United States there is a movement by some group of neo-Nazis to establish a white racialist "territorial sanctuary" somewhere in the Northwest;[12] not a new thing, actually, considering the other separatist and sectarian movements of long standing in the rest of the world. But is this how the nation of nations is to die, short of its "kosmic" promise? On the surface, this balkanization is presented as a comedy of decay; but the story line deals with the heroic efforts of one man to reverse it. He is Friday's employer, "the Boss," one Hartly Baldwin, the crusty likes of D. D. Harriman. For this purpose, he controls a cabal of sorts with the same iron-willed rule and idealism that Dee Dee exercises over Harriman Enterprises. The fans remember Baldwin in his younger days as the hero of the 1979 novella, "Gulf" (reprinted in *Assignment in Eternity*, 7–67).

"Gulf" (Milton's "gulf profound"?) is Heinlein's one story in a subgenre so typical that no master of Speculative Fiction can neglect trying his hand at it: the "superman" story. No doubt this derives

from the cult of the Samurai in Wells's *Modern Utopia* (1905), itself
a play on Plato's *Republic*. The distance between guardians and people
is the theme in both cases. Yet it is hard to think of more than one
or two critics who fail to recognize "Gulf" for what it is. Only these
few take it in evidence of what they imagine to be typical of Heinlein's
antidemocratic thought. Elsewhere his loyalty to American ideals, to the
denial of Platonic guardianship, is unmistakable.

The most pointed example of his constancy in this regard is the
early novella, "If This Goes On—," belonging to the Future History
series. Here the revolutionary elite of the Cabal that overthrows the
Prophet's theocracy, after three generations of reliance on the most
advanced techniques of mind conditioning, finally decides that their
original plan to recondition the American people to the idea of freedom
is not the way to restore the country's lost liberties. The deciding voice
in this debate is a revolutionary leader of some forty years experience
in the Cabal, pictured as "an angry Mark Twain" in his cantankerous,
white-haired old age. "Free men aren't conditioned!" he says. While it
is true that people had misused their franchise by voting for the First
Prophet, the only solution to the mess they got themselves into is to
restore their civil liberties, and let it go at that. "If they mess it up
again, that's their doing—but we have no right to operate on their
minds" (*PTT,* 572f.).

At any rate, Friday's Boss is given to the struggle for terrestrial unity,
lost cause as this turns out to be. As the instrument of salvation, he
spots the Shipstone Company as potentially the basis for a planetwide
government, not to say a systemwide government (with reference to all
the inhabited planets of the solar system). Friday's job is to find out
if that company can be influenced morally by the Boss's ideals. The
Shipstone Company, in all of its multinational and interplanetary sub-
sidiaries, deals in discrete units of packaged energy, devised by a
"basement inventor," Shipstone by name, who found a way to get
around the expensive problem of transmitting energy by long-distance
power lines. Unlike the murdered Dr. Pinero in "Life-Line," here is a
lone genius who has managed to prevail with his radically new invention.
Shipstone devices, large and small, are in use everywhere.

The Boss's plans are not altogether unreasonable. They follow up an
idea of H. G. Wells conceived in his *Open Conspiracy* (1928), which
was to persuade the heads of the world's great multinational corporations
to use the tentacular reach of their planetary business affairs for the
good of global unity. In the course of researching the Shipstone Company

for its moral and political potential, Friday is asked to look into "the marks of a sick culture."

After she has done her reading assignment in a book titled *The Last Days of the Sweet Land of Liberty,* the Boss asks her if she found any useful clues in it.

Yes sir. I did start making tallies. It is a bad sign when people of a country stop identifying themselves with the country and start identifying with a group. A racial group. Or a religion. Or a language. Anything, as long as it isn't the whole population. (*Friday,* 249)

To these examples of particularism she adds a number of others. Heinlein fans will be able to recall still others of like sort, the Moral Majoritarianism of "If This Goes On—" and the racialism of the Black Muslims in *Farnham's Freehold.* But her Boss interrupts to say she has overlooked the most important indicator.

Sick cultures show a complex of symptoms such as you have named . . . but a *dying* culture invariably exhibits personal rudeness. Bad manners. Lack of consideration for others in minor matters. A loss of politeness, of gentle manners, is more significant than a riot. (252)

Now the reader knows why the hero of *Cat* was so offended by bad manners on the Golden Rule habitat that he abandoned it. Built and occupied by a different breed of pioneering men and women, this off-Earth colony has itself decayed, as all frontiers do in time. Hence the need for unending frontiers, if the best in mankind is to reproduce itself indefinitely.

In Heinlein's judgment, rudeness is no small matter; bad manners indicate, as nothing else, a declining sense of civic obligation. As Lazarus Long says,

Moving parts in rubbing contact require lubrication to avoid excessive wear. Honorifics and formal politeness provide lubrication where people rub together. Often the very young, the untraveled, the naive, the unsophisticated deplore these formalities as "empty," "meaningless," or "dishonest," and scorn to use them. No matter how "pure" their motives, they thereby throw sand into machinery that does not work too well at best. (*LL,* 247f.)

It is not difficult to guess what Friday's Boss would make of a story appearing in the *New York Times* for 8 July 1986 and headlined,

"High Court Upholds School on Student's 'Vulgar' Talk." What he would find dismaying about it is the fact that it took a Supreme Court ruling (Bethel School District v. Fraser, No. 84–1667) to establish the most elementary duties of our school system to uphold the decencies of politesse.

The case involved a young boy who sued the authorities of his local high school for suspending him after his delivery of a "lewd and indecent" assembly speech, his defense being that his First Amendment rights to free speech had been violated. But Chief Justice Warren E. Burger, in a ruling that might well have been penned by a Heinlein viewpoint character, wrote that, "The schools, as instruments of the state, may determine that the essential lessons of civil, mature conduct cannot be conveyed in a school that tolerates lewd, indecent, or offensive speech and conduct such as that indulged in by this confused boy." In short, the right to free speech in the schools "must be balanced against the society's countervailing interests in teaching students the boundaries of socially appropriate behavior." Again, the manners are the morals. Education Secretary William J. Bennett said, "The decision reminds us that the schools must possess the moral authority to prepare our young people for citizenship."[13]

But in the end Friday's Boss (like the hero of *Cat*) is forced to surrender to the overwhelming incivil reality of things. Chivalry cannot be legislated. Therefore decent people will have to remove elsewhere, outside the system altogether; and so Friday is next assigned to research the costs and benefits of colonizing a new world out there in the great beyond. Herself benefiting from this project, Friday at last retires from her exotic business and settles for the pioneering life of a "colonial housewife," in a group marriage adapted to the conditions of a faraway frontier planet, short of females. There she completes the life-style of her namesake, Freya, the goddess of sexual license, marriage, and motherhood. For she had done not a little bed-hopping in the course of her duties, and her final group marriage is left to the reader to judge as licentious or not.

Moreover, her job also called now and again for the judicious assassination, unladylike as this may seem. But this is consistent with the heroine of "If This Goes On—," Sister Maggie, one of the Prophet's assigned Virgins. Joining the revolutionary Cabal, she does her job of killing for the cause in the Prophet's bedroom with a "vibroblade," then to settle down with the war hero John Lyle. But while Heinlein heroines are competent enough to be the equal of males in the dirty business of war and revolution, it is not really in their interest or that of the species to be so. As Lazarus Long says, "I've never felt that women should have to fight; it's a male's business to protect females and children. But a female should *be able* to fight because she may have to" (*TEL,* 178). In the end, Heinlein never violates his women-and-children-first rule (the basis of his alleged "sexism").

As for *Friday's* group marriage, that too is not inconsistent with Heinlein's traditional sense of morality (not so traditional, however, in the eyes of the Moral Majority, one of Heinlein's pet peeves). Insofar as he bases marriage on love, companionship, and care for children, he is all the more the absolutist of sexual ethics. Lazarus Long says,

Marriage is not something thought up by priests and inflicted on mankind; marriage is as much a part of mankind's evolutionary equipment as his eyes, and as useful to the race as eyes are to an individual. . . .

I am not speaking of monogamy; I mean *all* forms of marriage—monogamy, polyandry, plural and extended marriages with various frills. "Marriage" has endless customs, rules, arrangements. But it is "marriage" if-and-only-if the arrangement provides for children and compensates the adults. For human beings, the only acceptable compensation for the drawbacks of marriage lies in what men and women can give each other. (*TEL,* 194)

The critics who uniformly found *Friday* "sexist," mainly because of the heroine's licentious adventures, overlook it as a work of culture criticism. Friday's escapades are undertaken in a heroic and fighting cause, whose failure only draws attention to its object: how restore health to the sickness devitalizing this sweet land of liberty? The critics who choose to ignore this, while despising as ever Heinlein's unashamed patriotism, are themselves part of the problem. But not a large part. Heinlein's millions of fans, and new readers as well, much outweigh their influence. For he is arguably the most influential American writer of our day, as Twain was in his. And that is why this book is written, to help explain that large fact—one that cannot be wished away by Heinlein foes.

As Russia's greatest living poet, Yevgeny Yevtushenko, said in a daring speech at a Kremlin meeting of the 1986 Congress of the Union of Writers, "A writer without power is not a writer."[14] Yet the worst Heinlein critics can do is to demean his power and declare him a nonwriter. The following, just come to hand from one of the academy organs of the SFRA, is typical. Its editor rehearses once again "the

long lamentable case of Robert Heinlein, whose self-indulgent prose has
been hemorrhaging for decades, while no one in the industry could
muster the guts to apply a tourniquet. That timidity didn't hurt sales,
but it may very well have cost an important author a secure place in
the canons of the great."[15]

Chapter Seven
The Cave of Persecution

With *Time Enough for Love* (1973) the critics were at first baffled. But not for long. They soon rallied to a consensus, which has it that the old man really verged on senility with this one, "obsessed" with his own mortality because of a revived interest in the nearly immortal Lazarus Long, carried over from Heinlein's 1941 Future History novel, *Methuselah's Children*. In this, *Time Enough for Love* is taken to be a personal working out of the author's oedipal conflicts, especially since Lazarus Long himself is saved from dying only by his friends and relatives begging him to tell his life story, which centers on a love affair (via time travel) with his mother. More than one critical study pursued this line with all the learned apparatus of Freudian analysis, as if the author were rather more a sickly patient, self-indulgent in his dotage, than the vigorous master of his craft at the very height of his powers. Although Lazarus Long is a viewpoint character, as ever, it does not follow that he is autobiographical in any respect except for his opinions.

But what most baffles the critics is the question of form, in a debate that still goes on. How classify this most complex and lengthy thing Heinlein ever did? Some say that, in taxonomy, it belongs to the medieval romance, a collection of adventures revolving around a central character, with side stories developed around minor characters, as in the Arthurian romances. This is not unreasonable, in light of the four separate stories Lazarus Long tells about others in the course of reminiscing about himself. Others find it a loose and rambling narrative with no real structure at all. But some say it is epic in form. This happens to be correct, even though "epic" is routinely attached to every science-fiction novel of blockbusting size.[1] Yet in this case, the term is fitting.

The Greek *epos* was a long poem, or creative (poietic) work about history, and Homer was its ancient master. Heinlein is one of the few modern authors (apart from James Joyce with his *Ulysses*) to take the epic form seriously. *Time Enough for Love* is indeed Homeric, not in the least for its being advertised as "The capstone and crowning achievement of Heinlein's Future History."

The work is introduced by the Archivist Emeritus of the Howard Foundation who, in the name of the Howard Families of which Lazarus Long is the Senior, is obliged to collect all documents relating to his many lives and adventures; not alone his own remembrances of them, but also the mythic fables accreting to them, and not excluding the tales of the Senior's own fabulous storytelling. For the supernatural intervention of Homer's gods and goddesses, Heinlein has nonempirical things like rejuvenation, immortality, sentient computers, and time travel. These are standard science-fiction conventions, as were the supernatural elements in Homer standard to the *epos*. (Homer's Nestor was said by Ovid to have lived for more than two hundred years, while Phaon was rejuvenated by Venus.) For Homer's famous Catalogue of the Ships in the *Iliad*, there is the Notebooks of Lazarus Long, a catalogue of the Senior's opinions (recalling also the list of Shipstone companies in *Friday*, (241f.). For the adventures of the seafaring merchant trader Ulysses in the *Odyssey*, with his observations on distant places and peoples, there is Lazarus Long the roguish "sky merchant" (158). He is every bit the trickster hero his prototype is, "Ulysses of the many wiles."

Moreover, this episodic narrative has its unifying point of view, even as Homer had his. With him it was the heroic ethic, taught to all generations of heathen Greeks and Hellenized peoples before the advent of the Christian Bible. In *TEL* there is Heinlein's invincible horse sense, not unmixed with classical heroism and Spenserian gallantry, all reduced to that style of modern chivalry Walt Whitman celebrated as the American way of noblesse oblige. Or as even Kip the juvenile hero of *Have Space Suit—Will Travel* is exemplary enough to say, "it is better to be a dead hero than a live louse" (118). He lives up to his own motto, borrowed from that of the Chevalier de Bayard, *"sans peur et sans reproche"* (63). That is, he regards himself as a gentleman living "without fear and without reproach." What ethical influence Heinlein is destined to have in dignifying the now-fading American ideal of modern chivalry, beyond that claimed by readers in their millions worldwide, is impossible to measure. But it cannot be small, if only a fraction of the buyers of the fifty million copies of Heinlein books marketed to date regard the author as their "spiritual father." In this he makes felt his faith that America, in despite of her faults, is a force for good.

In a word, what Heinlein teaches (as voiced by Lazarus Long) is "that aggressive self-reliance necessary to a free human" (*TEL*, 197). But this is no license for incivility. The Heinlein individualist always acts the gentleman (both sexes implied) in the pink of courtesy; although when needed, he has reserves of superior cunning to draw upon. Once again, this is not the "rugged individualism" as the critics habitually read it. The rude and wolfish pursuit of self-interest is precisely what Heinlein brands as the mark of a sick and dying culture. With his brand of Emersonian self-reliance goes the responsibility to behave with self-discipline. This is the New World's distinction, as de Crèvecœur first observed, in its restoring of the ancient dignity of man to all men, when they are given the liberty under frontier conditions to act responsibly on their own, without coercive guidance from above. It is just such gentlemen who pioneer Heinlein's new frontiers when the old ones lapse (there will always be an Old World to be liberated from), above all Lazarus Long. To be sure, he likes to play up the wily side of his nature, as he does when asked to define that word "gentleman" he is wont to toss about in his conversation. In the past, he says, a gentleman was defined by his accidental birth among a feudal aristocracy,

that being a disparaging way of saying it was a trait genetically inherited. But that doesn't say what the trait is. A gentleman was supposed to prefer being a dead lion to being a live jackal. Me, I've always preferred to be a live lion, so that puts me outside the rules. Mmm . . . you could say in all seriousness that the quality tagged by that name represents the slow emergence in human culture of an ethic higher than simple self-interest— damn slow in emerging in my opinion; you still can't rely on it in a crunch. (*TEL,* 61)

So in the end, after joking about the question, Lazarus comes to the ethical heart of the matter: "simple self-interest" is uncivilized. Yet ironically, true self-interest, in de Crèvecœur's responsible and gentlemanly sense of the word, is a trait selected for only on those frontier wilds far from "civilization." But as the abuse of liberty springs eternal, even as freedom means the liberty to mess things up, civilization has no terminal destiny; it is always in the process of being refounded by a saving remnant of good and decent people—Gideon's band, or is it the Howard Families? Even so, Heinlein readers need not wait upon those new frontiers of outer space to pioneer if they are to fulfill the ethical instruction he imparts to them. They learn there is much for gentlemen and gentlewomen to do, by the force of their example, in holding the internal frontiers of our present civilization to account against

premature decay. Like all Spenserian cavaliers of the Faith, they are
expected to do their Father's work in a strange land.

Nor does *Time Enough for Love* lack the tragic note essential to the
epic form. It appears with touching force in "The Tale of the Adopted
Daughter" (chaps. 11 and 12), one of Lazarus Long's four divertisse-
ments, the so-called Dora sequence. The time for love in the book's
title is here combined with Heinlein's usual expertise in dramatizing
the adaptive know-how of the competent person, Whitman's gymnast.
In this case it is Lazarus Long's exploration and homesteading of a
frontier planet. He recollects that episode of his long-ago life in a
straightforward tale of settling a new land with little more than horses
and hand utensils. He tells of the daily joys and hardships of the
pioneer life as he experienced it. But more, Heinlein translates this
familiar experience of America's Western frontier into science fiction
with Lazarus Long's marriage to the "ephemeral" Dora, his wife of
normal lifespan. A story of mature sexual love handled with such
virtuosity that even the critics found it faultless, this episode gives the
novel a tragic note believable nowhere else in the science-fiction genre
but only in the *epos*.

Or again, Heinlein's treatment of incest is tragic enough in the
classical mold. Unlike today's working of that ancient theme, his is no
more pornographic than Sophocles', as Lazarus Long goes back in time
to the Kansas City of 1916, there and then to meet his mother and
have a passionate affair with her—four years after her son was born
Woodrow Wilson Smith in 1912. But maybe not so tragic after all.

A reporter from the *New Yorker,* interviewing Heinlein in 1974,
concluded that "the real hero of the book is not Lazarus Long but the
human germ plasm, which takes any available path to fulfill its built-
in program for survival."[2] It is true that the book contains a long
discourse on genetics (chap. 6, "The Tale of the Twins Who weren't"),
and this accords with the jacket copy. It says of Lazarus Long, "the
oldest man alive," that he is

to one degree or another the ancestor of most, if not all, of the planet he
inhabits in the galactic year 2053, which in Earth terms would be 4272.
That the planet itself [Secundus] is one not even suspected to exist when
the Senior is born is but one comment on the range of the story.

This range certainly is Darwinian in the evolutionary scope of its
perspective. But neither is it unrelated to Lazarus Long's individuality,

the singular traits of his unusual personhood. In filling up Secundus, the planet of his discovery and pioneering, with his own offspring, his expansive self on such a cosmic scale may be taken to embody a thought tried out by Ralph Waldo Emerson in his notebooks: "Then it seems to be true that the more exclusively idiosyncratic ["individual" deleted] a man is, the more infinite."[3]

Or better, the epic of Lazarus Long is a fitting gloss on Emerson's finished notion that "Every true man is a cause, a country; [he] requires infinite spaces and numbers and time fully to accomplish his design. . . . An institution is the lengthened shadow of one man." This from his 1841 essay on "Self-Reliance," but it might well have been said by his friend and correspondent Thomas Carlyle, in his book of essays published the same year, *On Heroes, Hero-Worship and the Heroic in History.* If Lazarus Long is the hero of Secundus, D. D. Harriman (for another example) is the shadow of a man lengthened in the Lunar Corporations he founded, which opened up those new frontiers of his Wonderful Dream.

Following after, it was Lazarus Long who led the Great Diaspora to the founding and peopling of Secundus (a second Earth). In this, Heinlein seems to play on that obscure "folk epic" by Vincent McHugh, *Caleb Catlum's America* (1936).[4] The acquisition date of Heinlein's copy is 1937, just two years before he began writing.

McHugh's novel tells the history of the Catlum family, who in the person of Caleb Catlum represents the history of America (Catlumville). Himself immortal, his relatives are every important person in the saga of the country's discovery and development, from Eric the Red, through Daniel Boone and Lewis and Clark, to Abraham Lincoln, including also mythic figures like Paul Bunyan and John Henry, not to mention Huck Finn and others from the pages of American literature. In the end, the Catlums are driven out of the freedom-loving land of their making by the Traders, those killers of the dream with their seeking of profits to no other purpose than the dictates of economic advantage alone. At that point, Caleb Catlum rallies his national family together, and in a long parade they all disappear under his leadership "into the Country of the Great Cave" (340), destined to reemerge in their faith we know not where.

The allusion here is to David's flight from Saul into the cave of Adullam in I Samuel 22:1-2, where it is written:

David departed from there and escaped to the cave of Adullam; and when his brothers and all his father's house heard it, they went down there to him. And every one who was in distress, and every one who was in debt, and every one who was discontented, gathered to him; and he became captain over them. And there were with him about four hundred men.

David, of course, came out again to triumph over Saul and to found a new and more righteous kingdom. Emerson, in referring to the same text, speaks of "the cave of persecution, which is the palace of spiritual power."[5] So too is the Country of the Great Cave a place of gathering spiritual power, wherein "grandpop" Catlum rallies his descendants, self-reliant Americans all. Likewise is Lazarus Long the grandpop or Senior of the Howard Families; he being the nearly immortal member of these long-lived families, they are by now (centuries later) all of them kinsmen by descent from his unfailing seed. It is they who people Secundus under his leadership, in their Great Diaspora out of their own cave of persecution, to which they have been driven by the unbearable failures of a dying Earth.

If *Caleb Catlum's America* is the nation's spiritual autobiography, reduced to the family history of Catlumville, *TEL* is the future history of the human race, reduced to the personal narrative of Lazarus Long, as he relates his own adventures and those of his cosmic progeny. In this, the novel also has affiliations with George R. Stewart's *Man: An Autobiography* (1946), the anthropological drama of the ages told in the first person. The works of Stewart are well known to fans, writers, and critics alike, if only because his one science-fiction novel, *Earth Abides* (1949), received the first International Fantasy Award of 1951. This, too, is human autobiography, the story of Ish (whose Hebrew name means "man" in the collective sense), the last civilized American to survive a pandemic disease that nearly depopulates the nation, the whole world, in fact, which is to be repopulated for a fresh start in large part by his own children and grandchildren; he is the "grandpop" of a new and vigorous race of frontiersmen reduced to extreme conditions, as they recommence the human adventure, starting once again from its primitive beginnings.[6]

From *Time Enough for Love* it is an easy turn to *Job: A Comedy of Justice* (1984), whose hero is the very personification of the persecuted. It is also the one Heinlein novel that both fans and critics are united in praising (as *I Will Fear No Evil* was the one they agreed to disparise). What the critics like about it especially is its "liberal" stand against

Moral Majority, Inc., whose conservatism they loathe even more than Heinlein's. Taking their cue not so much from the book's innate quality as from its being denounced from the pulpits of the nation's fundamentalist churches, their satisfaction rests mainly with its mockery of the Moral Majority's political program (*Job,* 149f.). Yet its hero, a fundamentalist minister, is treated with abiding sympathy.

He is the Reverend Alexander Hergensheimer, who learns the lesson of patience as did the biblical Job, in facing up to persecution without getting paranoid about his lot. Or as Alex himself puts it, he learned "to face calmly the ancient mysteries of life, untroubled by my inability to solve it" (67). As with the original Job, the jacket copy reads, "Something was out to get him!" This something is none other than Jehova, out to test Job to the limits of human endurance, but using modern methods. The troubles visited upon Alex and his wife Margrethe are created by illusion, with the aid of "hollow grams" on a continental scale, so that the couple seem to be switched from one parallel world to another, in confusing succession. No sooner do they manage to adapt to each variant of American culture and history, as they start out each time from scratch at dishwashing and tablewaiting, than they are switched again. But they stand together always, as loving husband and wife, and as friends and comrades in hardship and poverty. This last, after all, is no illusion. As the biblical Job was deprived of all his possessions, Alex also is—over and over again. Worst of all, Alex is bereft of his wife at the Day of Judgment (something his former ministry gave much thought to), and he is swept up in the Rapture into Heaven without her.

Alex enters the Holy City of scriptural imagery, together with countless millions of other souls, in a lengthy episode of sustained comedy. The Holy City and its administration under St. Peter is made concrete to the last practical detail required for such a celestial bureaucracy. A few glimpses of it are foreshadowed in *Stranger in a Strange Land* (chapters 28 and 30), but the conception as a whole in *Job* is a hilarious improvement upon that rendered by Mark Twain in "Capt. Stormfields's Visit to Heaven" (in *Report from Paradise,* 1909), itself an irreverent play on that Puritan classic, Michael Wigglesworth's *Day of Doom* (1662). In search of his wife, Alex wangles an interview with St. Peter, whose office records show that Margrethe is nowhere present in Heaven; and so God arranges for Alex to visit the other place, run by His brother. Alex there appeals to Lucifer who, after switching off Hell's holographic scenery, explains that Jehova used the same means in playing

His dirty tricks. Impressed by Alex's fortitude, he reveals that the loss of Margrethe was not his doing, not even Jehova's, but that of a Scandinavian god, Loki, belonging to Margrethe's own mythological heritage. And so Lucifer offers to visit a higher power they all work for, Koshchei by name. Koshchei turns out to be helpful because he is annoyed by Jehova's unpaid-off bet with Loki. The latter had wagered that Jehova in His favorite game would fail to break Alex as He had all the others.

Koshchei "the deathless" in Russian folklore is "a bony, emaciated old man, rich and wicked, who knows the secret of eternal life."[7] But here he figures as one of those hierarchical creators of the cosmos, whose nature is revealed to be not so much evil as amoral (as the universe itself is from the Darwinian standpoint).

Wearing that same aspect, Koshchei appears in a work by James Branch Cabell, *Jurgen: A Comedy of Justice* (1921), whose very subtitle is echoed in *Job: A Comedy of Justice*. In Cabell's novel Koshchei is "he who makes things as they are," a phrase derived from a line in Kipling's poem of 1892, "When Earth's Last Picture is Painted." It is Jurgen's lesson to accept things as they are, during the course of his search for his loved one, which takes him on a grand tour of Heaven and Hell, and all other countries the human imagination has conceived as lying in between. Only afterward does Jurgen return with a sigh of relief to that real existence that alone is tolerable to the human spirit. This, finally, is a twist on Kipling, whose concluding lines to the poem in question go,

> And only the Master shall praise us and only the
>   Master shall blame;
> And no one shall work for money, and no one shall
>   work for fame;
> But each for the joy of working, and each, in his
>   separate star,
> Shall draw the Things as he sees it for the God of
>   Things as They are!

The twist is, Jurgen does indeed have his individual star, but he frees himself from living for praise or blame by the Master, who is the "Master of All Good Workmen." While Jurgen's chivalry is itself a product of the Master's own work, it lies beyond His judgment and understanding. If, as Emerson says, "Every true man is a cause" (as Jurgen reveals himself to be), then the human spirit at its best is a better example of self-reliance than is the divine image from which it was struck off.

Jurgen at first had found the universe unfair; there was no justice in it. But at last he learns to accept things as they are. The idea of theodicy, a vindication of God's divine justice, beyond human concepts of fairness or unfairness, is illusory. Not to appreciate that the universe is amoral is "the comedy of justice" for both Cabell and Heinlein. But there is this added comic element, the biggest cosmic joke of all. The God of Christian theology is real enough (as is Loki, it seems), but He is no lone divinity, alone in the creation business. Jehova, copartner with the Prince of Hell, is but one of many understrappers and jobbers in the business of cosmic construction, under a hierarchy of architects. Jurgen and Alex alike find Koshchei located somewhere between God and some higher authorities of infinite regress, whose infinitude (the ultimate Master of Nature) is represented by Heinlein in the Masonic name for "the Great Architect" (*Job,* 344).[8]

And so Alex in his quest for Margrethe learns "to accept the universe as it is, rather than try to force it into some preconceived shape" (*Job,* 101), that is, into some theodicy. In due course he gets her back from a strange frozen limbo, thanks not to any fairness of divine justice but to the chancy outcome of debate among the Great Architect's underlings. Lucifer (whose terrestrial name is Jerry) takes Alex to meet Koshchei. It is the latter, in his normal-looking lawyer's office constructed for the occasion somewhere in the grayness of nowhere space, who chairs that debate between Jerry (Lucifer) and his brother Jehova, the two of them being coequals in their assigned business (at a very local level) of dealing with mankind. Jerry presents his case for his client Alex. In the end, Koshchei appeals to a higher power and Alex's wife is restored to him.

Jerry's case is pleaded on the grounds that his client, this lowly human creature Alex, had withal withstood the experiment done upon him. Yahweh (speaking in a humorous Yiddish idiom) wonders why Jerry should concern himself, since all humans are equally toys of playful contempt. This view is not a little defensive, however, as God tries to get out of His bad debt to Loki. (It is he who holds Margrethe in limbo until he collects; else he takes her to Valhalla.)

Jerry turns to Koshchei by way of reply, carefully sidestepping the delicate issue of God's pawnshop mentality.

Mr. Chairman, almost everything about a human creature is ridiculous, except in its ability to suffer bravely and die gallantly for whatever it loves and believes in. The validity of that belief, the appropriateness of that love, is irrelevant; it is the bravery and gallantry that count. These are uniquely human qualities, independent of mankind's creator, who has none of them himself—as I know, since he is my brother . . . and I lack them, too. (*Job*, 438f.)

In fine, that uniquely human thing (at least in the best of mankind) is the power of volition. Come what may from the fates, the will to endure is all. As William Faulkner said in his acceptance speech for the Nobel Prize in Literature for 1950, "man will not only endure; he will prevail . . . because he has a soul and a spirit of compassion and sacrifice." And he added, "the writer's duty is to write about these things." This Heinlein does in his own way, while yet reaching a much wider audience, although it would be impossible to guess from the critical literature.

Likewise does Jurgen defend himself against the powers that be by "snapping his fingers" at them, for their foolishness in creating a world order in which its human animals turn out to be objects of envy for all their lowliness. No wonder Jurgen defies the game rigged against him. So, too, does Alex. It is what invites Lucifer to take him on as a client in a policy dispute with his bothersome brother Jehova.

Lucifer (Jerry) complains that Jehova, in running His "destruction test" on Alex had, as a matter of artistic principle, failed to do His creature the "kindness" of treating him consistently. Koshchei moderates the dispute by putting in, "to insist on kindness would be to eliminate that degree of freedom for which volition in creatures was invented. Without the possibility of tragedy the volitionals might as well be golems." Asked to amplify, he says that the "guild rules" of creation do not exclude tragedy, only such inconsistency of treatment in a game so rigged that the "creatures cannot win." Jerry concedes the point, now able to say why his Hell keeps on getting all those "losers" of Yahweh's dirty game. Then Koshchei goes on: "For a creature to act out its own minor part, the rules under which it must act must be either known to it or be such that the rules can be known through trial and error—with error not always fatal. In short the creature must be able to learn and to benefit by its experience" (429f.).

Koshchei finally prevails upon higher powers to restore Margrethe to Alex (she had been recumbent there all along encased in a block of ice on Koshchei's desk); but in doing this they have done nothing to alter their guild rules, and surely they never would be disposed to do so for the sake of such a minor piece of artwork as one of their human products. Theirs is no act of special generosity; it but scores a point against one of their demigodly rule-breakers. Yahweh, however, is likely to pay no heed after this is done and settled.

So it is left to the likes of Lazarus Long to observe, "certainly the game is rigged. Don't let that stop you; if you don't bet, you can't win" (*LL*, 240). One of Bret Hart's frontier gamblers has the same to say: "With him life was at best an uncertain game, and he recognized the usual percentage in favor of the dealer." (In a curious way, it is denial of truth that makes men free). Such is the gallantry of the human "volitional," that he defies the gods who made him; all the while they themselves are made to look the more foolish because they misunderstand him, the very source of their uneasy envy. How else does Alex find his one great truth? It is the Summum Bonum of his chivalrous quest, the winning back of his wife and companion from the "unfair" doings of the amoral cosmos. This is justice enough for him, accepting things as they are in her company. "Heaven is where Margrethe is" (*Job*, 439). The critics, however, could not help faulting Heinlein for this ending, which they described as a sinful display of uxoriousness (following Milton's dislike of wife-worship). The old man proved himself once again to be "self-indulgent" (a standard complaint among SFRA academics).

Job is one of Heinlein's masterful adult novels, all the more so because it makes such creative use of the works of Cabell and Twain. Literature builds on literature; and there is no lack of originality in the way Heinlein has assimilated these classics to his purpose. But he is no less apt in building on his own previous work, as he did in his next novel.

The Cat Who Walks through Walls (1985) may be tagged as a sequel to *The Moon is a Harsh Mistress* (1966), which became a cult book of the libertarian movement with the same unexpected impact that *Stranger in a Strange Land* had on the youth movement. Indeed, the libertarians picked up on the slogan of the New American Revolution for lunar independence that the novel tells about, and made it their slogan. It is TANSTAAFL!, the acronym for "There ain't no such thing as a free lunch." Both fans and critics take this to be one of Heinlein's word coinages, like "free fall," "astrogation," "grok," and "waldo." This is not so, however. It was, Heinlein confides, an ironic saying of the socialist movement during the Depression years, when he himself went through a "socialist phase," thus prompting him to run on the Democratic and not the Republican ticket when he entered California politics in 1938. But the TANSTAAFL idea, after all, is a very ancient one of no particular ideological import, going back to a witticism of one Fulminous Minor of the Augustan Age, who said, *Non existat prandium gratuitum* (literally, "there exists no such thing as a freely bestowed noon refreshment").

At all events, TANSTAAFL is the slogan of lunar independence, while it is also a warning to all who would venture upon the frontier conditions of the moon in ignorance of this precept. For the moon is indeed a "harsh mistress," in keeping with its hazards. "Luna has only one way to deal with a new chum: Either he makes not one fatal mistake, in personal behavior [rudeness, for example] or in coping with the environment that will bite without warning . . . or he ends up as fertilizer in a tunnel farm" (*Moon*, 201). The same goes for Luna in its later and more developed condition, as described in *Cat*. Its wild frontier has been tamed to a certain extent by its colonists, but its environment still bites the would-be freeloader. Or better, its pioneers are ready to bite the newcomer unaware of its basic rule: every citizen of Luna pays his own way, or else. No free lunch. Only the moonstruck Loonies are given to know this in their hearts.

The same precept applies to the Golden Rule habitat, later put up in lunar orbit. One of its unhappy newcomers from Earth, known only as Bill, thinks the habitat owes him a living (the way things are "dirtside"). He resents having to pay his air fee, and this is discussed by an older resident, one of the novel's viewpoint characters (the Pixel-keeping heroine, in fact), in the following terms:

Bill has the socialist disease in its worst form; he thinks the world owes him a living. He told me—sincerely—smugly!—that of *course* everyone was entitled to the best possible medical and hospital service—free of course, unlimited of course, and of course the government would pay for it. He couldn't even understand the mathematical impossibility of what he was demanding. But it's not just free air and free therapy, Bill honestly believes that anything *he* wants must be possible . . . and should be free. (*Cat*, 202; ellipsis in the original)

The same mathematical realities hold for spaceship Earth. If they be disregarded the whole planet is become a cave of persecution, ruined by a rude insistence on rights (personal or sectarian) over duties.

That is why *The Cat Who Walks through Walls* takes for its ironical subtitle yet another one drawn from a Cabell novel: "A Comedy of Manners." Indeed, almost all of Cabell's novels have subtitles dealing with a comedy of this or that. One of them is "A Comedy of Wife-Worship," which is in fact a praise of monogamy. Likewise is *Cat* actually a celebration of good manners, even though the subtitle suggests a playful treatment of them. The point is that manners, domestic or civil, are too important to be taken seriously; they must be appreciated with a sense of humor because they do seem, on the surface, to be arbitrary and absurd. But ignoring them is more tragic than observing them is comic.

Chapter Eight
Calvinist Mythology

Like Mark Twain, Heinlein is a determinist but unlike him no arch-pessimist. Twain asks, "Was the World Made for Man?" His answer is no, while Heinlein's is a qualified yes (he being a short-term pessimist and long-run optimist). Twain's gloomy question is raised in a collection of posthumous writings, *Letters from the Earth,* edited by Bernard De Voto in 1962. These include a long essay on "The Damned Human Race"; the adjective in that grim title is no mere expletive. The Great Humorist here reveals his latent scorn for mankind, as he did early in his career when he described humanity as but a "hackful of reptiles." It comes out again in his short story of 1900, "The Man that Corrupted Hadleyburg." The town's leading men prove to be dishonest without exception, and their only defense is that their corruption is "Ordered! Oh, everything's ordered."

Whether or not determinism is a valid philosophy, it normally is bad doctrine for the writer of fiction because ordinary people do not feel that their lives are predetermined. Twain gets around this problem in *Huckleberry Finn* by allowing the boy's river adventure to be his free-will experience, while to the author the Mississippi is taken for the all of human existence, a symbol of the collective journey. But Heinlein's heroes are not ordinary people, and they often act as conscious agents of human destiny. For them, when they talk about it, the paradox of free will and necessity is resolved by their volunteering to assist destiny and give the inevitable a helpful push.

There is behind this viewpoint the same Calvinist mythology of determinism that strongly influenced Twain. Both Missouri authors were raised under Bible-Belt Methodism, taken inland to the Midwest from its New England beachhead established by our Pilgrim forefathers. Heinlein says his cradle religion was the Methodist Discipline of 1904, and he vividly recalls the rigor of its details. No card playing, for instance; he was allowed a deck of cards as a youngster only for doing magic tricks, never for playing games. No liquor, of course, and he learned dancing only after entering the Naval Academy where, as it happens, he became (in the supreme art of dancing) its champion swordsman (a feat celebrated in *Glory Road*, in which Heinlein proved himself master of yet another genre, the sword-and-sorcery novel).

At all events, he broke with his cradle religion at the age of thirteen (keeping this matter to himself) when he discovered the two great works of Charles Darwin, *The Origin of Species* (1859) and *The Descent of Man* (1871). Thereafter he lost his "bigoted" faith in the King James version of "the literal word of God." Yet he continues to speak about "the nature of Man and his Destiny" and of "*Cosmic Purpose* as a 'least hypothesis' for the universe" (*EU*, 545, 312, 383). In his personal liberation Heinlein thus retraces the history of secularized Calvinism, whose two original exponents were Thomas Carlyle in England and Emerson in America, both men sharing their insights through correspondence and mutual visits.

Carlyle (1795–1881), however, seems to better exemplify Heinlein's version of it because he took Darwinism into account as Emerson did not. For Carlyle (who had studied for the Calvinist ministry before he broke with its theology), the providential God of the Above had become the evolutionary God of the Ahead; the elect of Heaven had become world-historical figures collaborating in the unfinished work of Creation. Not a terminal Heaven calls mankind to the fulfillment of its cosmic purpose, but some open-ended Future.[1] Man's destiny is to move forward in accord with some unfolding evolutionary plan, whose historical "Great Men" are its instruments. D. D. Harriman, in opening up the new frontiers of outer space, is one such conscious agent, and Heinlein explicitly compares him with a Carlyle hero (*PTT*, 185).

This comparison is faithfully carried out in "The Man Who Sold the Moon." Like his namesake, Harriman believes that with great wealth goes great responsibility. So it is up to him to finance the Wonderful Dream—"the biggest thing for the human race since the discovery of fire" (*PTT*, 146). Indeed, his being "so obsessed with the Wonderful Dream" (170) is his mark of grace. At one with Carlyle's heroes of historical progress, his every trickery is justified, ruthless to do what he must in the cause of human advancement, in that he is given divine insight into the inevitable drift of things. "We've got to guess which way things are moving, give them a boost," Harriman says to his associates. "Our race is about to burst forth to the planets; if we've got the initiative God promised an oyster we will help it along!" Or again: "It's coming, it's coming soon, whether we touch it or not" (124, 130, 146). But he alone is elected by destiny for the task because in no other hands will the benefits of space flight be developed for the good of all mankind; as an American capitalist belonging to this nation of nations, he sees to it that a monopoly on these benefits is refused to the advantage of the other superpower and its aggressive, war-risking designs. "I plan to be the Man in the Moon myself—and give it my personal attention to see that it is handled right" (146). The institution of space travel on the basis of free enterprise, in Harriman's Lunar Corporations, is indeed the lengthened shadow of one man, to recall Emerson's phrase; or to say the same thing in the language of Carlyle, he is a world-historical Great Man responsive to the pull of the Future.

Heinlein's Calvinism without theology is therefore no less informed than Carlyle's by those Five Points of doctrine formulated by John Calvin himself. Calvin (1509–1564) is one of the great theologians with Martin Luther in the making of the Protestant Reformation, whose theology shaped the ideas of the Puritans in England and through them the religious culture of the early American colonies, from which a number of sectarian derivatives migrated westward to influence the Methodism of Heinlein's upbringing.

The Five Points were hammered out by Calvin at the Synod of Dort, in 150 sessions between 1618 and 1619.[2] (In those days, theological summitry among great religious leaders was as important as today's political summitry, carried on with the same ideological fervor.) As headlined in the original text, they are as follows (with my summary of them):

1. Unconditional election. God has predestined all events to His purpose, having from the beginnings of the world selected those to be saved in Heaven and those renegades to be lost in Hell.

2. Irresistible grace. Salvation is foreordained by God, never as a reward for good works. The elect can neither win nor lose the gift of grace by their own acts.

3. Total depravity. The Fall has left man in a state of corruption and helplessness; no bootstrap operations are possible. The damned can no more lift themselves out of Hell than can the elect raise themselves to Heaven.

4. Limited atonement. Christ on the Cross earned God's forgiveness, or grace, only for the elect. They do not choose but are chosen to do the saving work of God's purpose.

5. The perseverance of the saints. God preserves his elect or saints, in despite of their general sins. He renews them in their good works, given them to do in the first place. "Say not in thy heart: My strength and the power of my hand has wrought this great wonder; but thou

shalt remember the Lord thy God, for He it is who gives the strength to do great deeds" (Deuteronomy 8:17).

This is pretty tough doctrine, and it may be wondered how anyone could live with it, believing that everything was predetermined anyhow. So why bother doing good works? Are we not, then, but agents of the inevitable?

But look closer. For our Puritan ancestors this was a fighting doctrine for movers and doers, not a passive one for societal dropouts, letting history take its own course. If our ancestors were merely agents, they were at least the agents of forces that guaranteed achievements greater than their own frail personal efforts ever could have brought about. Or as Lazarus Long says, "Maybe Jesus was right when he said that the meek shall inherit the earth—but they inherit very small plots, about six feet by three" (*TEL,* 158: see also *Number of the Beast,* 508). The emphasis here is on God, or Cosmic Purpose, not on Christ or a personal salvation figure.

Moreover, doctrinal beliefs are not the all of religion. There are social and political dimensions as well. As it happens, the Reformation coincided with the so-called Bourgeois Revolution, when European merchants were no longer content to restrict their expanding business activity for the sake of conforming to the leveling ethic of Catholic doctrine. The chief tenet of the established church at that time was that work (sweat of the brow, etc.) was a God-inflicted punishment for mankind's Original Sin in the Fall (alluded to in point 3). But the Protestants redefined work (business and trade included) as a divine calling, as the doing of God's mysterious purpose. This is the familiar thesis of the German sociologist, Max Weber, in his *Protestant Ethic and the Spirit of Capitalism* (1920). What Weber missed, however, was the Reformation's hidden premise. This was left for the later German sociologist Helmut Shoeck to bring out, in a book of 1966 quite simply titled, *Envy.*[3]

Shoeck argues that Calvinism did much to create a new climate of fraternal faith and work, in which the businessman was able to play the growing market economy for personal gain and wealth, without inciting envy on the part of his fellow citizens. He was now immune from jealous resentment and could flex his economic genius without fear or shame. His material success was no longer an object of malice, directed at his personal worth by the less ambitious, now it was only a matter of luck in God's election lottery; ambition and competence and hard work had nothing to do with it. The inequalities of human capacity at last got a religious rationale, putting off the envy-loaded, egalitarian doctrine of Catholic theology. The rich man who formerly could no more enter Heaven than a camel pass through the eye of a needle, was himself now a living saint. (So he always was, if the eye of the needle in the biblical text be construed as one of the gateways of ancient Jerusalem, low and narrow, called Needle Gate, getting through which obliged the rich man's pack-laden camel to bow in deference to the social responsibilities of his wealth.) His work now was God's work, a calling and a vocation; and if only a few were capable of such enterprise, then the community as a whole must benefit from his talent—all ships rising equally on the tide of that economic development he stimulated, to use a metaphor popularized by President Kennedy.

Lazarus Long has a word or two to say on this head when he remarks, "Throughout history, poverty is the normal condition of man. Advances which permit this norm to be exceeded—here and there, now and then—are the work of an extremely small minority. . . . Whenever this tiny minority is kept from creating . . . the people then slip back into abject poverty" (LL, 244; ellipses mine). It is evident from this quotation that Heinlein fully appreciates the practicalities of the Protestant work ethic. When productive genius is kept in check, the result is a failed economy. But the so-called problem of economic underdevelopment is really a political as it once was a religious problem, as is the case today wherever Marxism holds innovative wealth-making hostage to the green eyes of envy—this in the name of a class-war ideology that is no more progressive than was the Catholicism of medieval Europe.

The European miracle that was the Bourgeois Revolution, the world's first case of economic takeoff, may very well owe everything to a solution of the envy problem made by Calvinism.[4] The assertive individual was given his head without regard for the leveling taboos of "social justice," and all they entail for the bleak history of socialism and its redistributive ideals.

Or as Heinlein states the problem, "Some people insist that 'mediocre' is better than 'best'. They delight in clipping wings because they themselves can't fly. They despise brains because they have none. Ptah!" So speaks the father of Pewee, the bright young heroine of Have Space Suit—Will Travel. She herself says, "I can't help being a genius."[5]

Taking no unsocial pride in this indubitable quality, she is aware that it is owing to her luck in the genetic lottery, being the child of two highly endowed parents (see HSS, 175, 251). She simply is one of God's elect (or better, the darling of Cosmic Purpose), as is her sixteen-year old boyfriend, Kip, of similar heritage. After incredible adventures in the world-saving business, which was their lot not quite by chance to undertake, Kip says of Pewee, "she was gallant and loyal and smart—and she had guts" (*HSS*, 250). This comes out as Kip, the teenage narrator of the story, tells how they saved the day at the very dock of doom, before a tribunal of monstrous aliens, whose collective life is unified by the perfect harmony of its impersonal and equally replaceable parts. Brought before this universal bar of social justice, the two kids are indicted for the "savagery" of their race's fighting spirit. The trial is rigged from the start, yet Kip somehow blurts out the right words that give the alien judges pause. After sentencing planet Earth to extinction for its possible long-term threat to galactic order in their part of the universe, the judges offer Kip and Pewee sanctuary in thanks for their testimony. But at Pewee's prompting, Kip says in effect, thanks but no thanks; we'd rather be returned home to die with our own kind.

That does it. The aliens, implacable monsters of socialist logic, are puzzled by this absurd folly of human heroism and its illogical capacity for self-sacrifice. Chivalry is beyond their understanding; that these two representatives of the human race should throw away their lives for the sake of others not nearly as gallant as they—what a mystery! How can it be that Kip and Pewee, a test sample of humanity, are so unlike what they are supposed to represent? Even Kip himself wonders why his impulsive remark turned the trick. Turning to Pewee after the reprieve is given, he says, " 'Die trying' is the proudest human thing" (237), thus revealing what a resource the human race has in its elect. It's just what the aliens lack, the whole race of them damned because not any one of them is different enough to be a saint.

The element of determinism in Kip's unpremeditated defense of humankind, not in the least thought out on his part, sorts with a saving speech once made by Huck Finn. Finding himself in a tight spot, although far from cosmic in scope, he reflects on his uncanny ability to get out of it.

I went right along, not fixing up any particular plan, but just trusting in Providence to put the right words in my mouth when the time came; for I'd noticed that Providence did put the right words in my mouth, if I left it alone." (*Huckleberry Finn*, chap. 32)

No less does Heinlein teach the same lesson, and with undisguised intent especially in his juveniles, as in *Have Space Suit—Will Travel*. Kip and Pewee exemplify the author's Calvinistic message at his most explicit, and his readers are not slow to catch on.

What they learn from Heinlein is that precocity is no affront to our nation's democratic ideals. When he says, "I don't write for stupid people," his readers know what he means without being told in so many words. The hidden advice is: Don't you ever feel ashamed of your superior competency. It is providential. So don't let the envious tear you down. Otherwise you are stopped from doing good works. That is the lesson of American chivalry.

But more. While Kip and Pewee are kids with the right stuff, innate to their character as it is to all Heinlein heroes juvenile or adult, they are also models of studied attainment. Elsewhere Heinlein speaks of education's "three-legged stool of understanding [which] is upheld by *history, language,* and *mathematics.* Equipped with these you can learn anything you want to learn. But if you lack *any* one of them you are just another ignorant peasant with dung on your boots" (*EU,* 519). Kip and Pewee are no less exemplary for having done their homework in these fields. They are not merely bright kids, they have worked hard to cultivate their natural gifts. Their bantering dialogue exhibits an easygoing at-homeness with Heinlein's three-legged stool of understanding. They know astronomy and the engineering sciences as well, combined with a familiarity with technical things and an ability to improvise under stress (Kip's mating of his airbottle to Pewee's pressure suit, during their trek on the moon, when the two systems do not properly match). Their knowledge of history always is on display, American history in particular and including scientific history (they know who the lunar craters and research station are named after). Also notable is their unassuming readiness to quote from literary classics (Shakespeare, Edward Young, Cervantes), and it is clear they know Latin and French. (Heinlein is all for restoring Latin, especially, to the high school curriculum.) Kip in addition knows musical notation, which he (as narrator) uses in his account to record the tonal qualities of alien speech.

The two of them are gymnastic indeed, in Walt Whitman's meaning of the word. But their learned abilities amount to nothing if not united with their innate disposition to the higher values of duty and loyalty, which they have been selected for by fate to demonstrate. Character of that sort is rare, and Heinlein teaches his readers to appreciate it. So the Calvinistic lesson is: Think of your abilities as a gift of grace. Be self-confident in them, yet not prideful, and your competence is proof against envy.

Or as Lazarus Long says, "if you don't like yourself, you *can't* like other people" (*LL,* 242). Nor help them. Indeed, this near-immortal says, "If a person had time enough, he could love all that majority who are decent and just" (*TEL,* 248). As for the others, they have their damnation certified in the long run, as do the elect their sainthood.

But then again, the ability to apply oneself is itself a mark of grace in the Protestant work ethic. This is brought out plainly enough in *Methuselah's Children* (1941), in which Lazarus Long leads his first expedition of the Howard Families to another planet. In this case they were forced to leave Earth because their genetically inbred capacity for long life had become the object of vicious envy on the part of the majority of humans, given by nature only a normal lifespan; democratic mobs insist that the Terran government do something about it, either kill off the Howard Families or force them to reveal their "secret" to all. Having no secret to share, other than a natural inequality, the families flee certain destruction.

Among other places their starship lands on is the planet of the Little People. A Lotus Land this place is, with its placid seas, low hills, and calm breezes, where even porkchops will grow on trees if you so desire. Or at least they will bear such tasty fruit, and much else, at the command of the Little People who inhabit this place. They are "masters in the manipulation of life forms" (*PTT,* 800). Moreover, they are willing to share their powers with the visiting Earthman. But the catch is, this requires their going native, so to speak, by sinking their personalities into the local form of social life. The Little People are telepathic beings, living in rapport with each other, in groups of from thirty to ninety individuals who share a group soul. As Lazarus Long observes, "collectively, each rapport group constituted a genius that threw the best minds the Earthmen had to offer into the shade" (*PTT,* 805). They have only to "think" a plant into being and there it is, beyond any powers of human biotechnology. But each unit in these rapport groups is moronic; they contain no individual egos, no "cranky individualists" as in the human condition (815). They rather possess a group ego, immortal and undying, in which there is neither death nor selfhood. Lazarus thinks the place no more than "a well-run zoo" (803), and advises the families to remove, as Captain Ulysses advised his men to leave Homer's original Lotus Land. But some wish to stay and go native (as did some under Ulysses), and so did Mary Sperling, nearing old age and death: "Faced with the eternal problem of life and death, she had escaped the problem by choosing neither . . . selflessness. She had found a group willing to receive her, she had crossed over" (*PTT,* 806; ellipsis in the original). It's not the sort of thing Lazarus Long wants for himself or other of his families. To give up individuality to this "timeless snug harbor of ease," he thinks, is "to give up whatever it was that made them *men*" (805). To him, "it did not seem like a safe path for humans" (801). One of his close associates agrees. "Damn it, I want to *work* for my living!" (809). And so the strong-minded depart, leaving the rest behind. The weak fall to a lazy selflessness, while the chosen of destiny move on to advance the human race. Such is the function of any frontier situation, to sort out the elect from the nonelect. Or as Lazarus Long says elsewhere, "migration always involves selection and improvement" (*TEL,* 12).

But while such a Calvinistic line of interpretation looks plausible, there is more than one stumbling block. Quite apart from the fact that Heinlein resisted it during my visit with him, I myself have some theological trouble with it. Yet there is a possible way out. Most men for Heinlein are good and decent (for all their failings at the ballot box, when duped by demagogues), as they are not in Twain's very strict reading of Calvinist doctrine, in which the elect are so few, the damned so many. Thus only a pitiful few are called upon to do God's work.

Twain carries over the pagan view of heathen antiquity, for whom Bias of Prie'nē (one of the Seven Sages of Greece) was a spokesman when he said, "most men are bad." But St. Augustine, on whom Calvin mainly relies, has it that a great middle ground of good people exists between the elect and the damned, although their postmortal fate, Heaven or Hell, is not indicated (unless they are reserved for Purgatory, the in-between resting place calibrated by later Catholic doctrine). Unlike Twain's determinism, pagan in its pessimistic view of suffering humanity, unchanged and unchanging through the ages, Heinlein's is more optimistic. Grounded in good Augustinian doctrine, he allows that man's everlasting progress, inching upward to the light, is assured in the predetermined quantity of the decent added to the elect. And while destiny for Heinlein has no terminal point in Heaven above, it does have a Future ahead to look forward to.

Movement toward a higher ethic, going beyond "simple self-interest," is just what Lazarus Long expects, no matter how slow in coming.

What else can be the ethical meaning of those new frontiers of outer space opened by Harriman Enterprises?

> Out ride the sons of Terra,
> Far drives the thundering jet,
> Up leaps the race of Earthmen.
> Out, far, and onward yet.

So sings the blind poet of the spaceways in "The Green Hills of Earth" (*PTT*, 373). The purpose of man, in his unfolding evolutionary adventure, is to become a *Citizen of the Galaxy,* to cite Heinlein's juvenile title of 1957. It is a title that echoes a phrase coined by Voltaire, in his *Philosophical Dictionary* (1764). There it figures as a cosmic outlook on the nature of things, from which it can be seen that no conflict exists between private interest and public interest.

Heinlein's reading of galactic citizenship, however, is quite literal, the mark of the First Human Civilization to come. But it will come about only after a tough selective process that brings out the best in humanity. Man is prepared to endure in this purpose because the species has its elect in the service of the human cause. At the same time, Heinlein cautions his perceptive readers not to boast of their competency, if they are to accept their true calling in this racial drama. St. Paul, in a text crucial to Calvinist theology, says, "For it is not the man who commends himself that is accepted, but the man whom the Lord commends" (II Corinthians, 10:18). St. Paul also said, in a text cited by St. Augustine and John Calvin alike, "Who made you different? What have you got that you did not first receive? If you have received all this, why glory in it as if you had not been given it?" (I Corinthians, 4:7). Or as Lazarus Long says, "Never frighten a little man. He'll kill you" (*LL*, 347).

To be sure, Lazarus Long fears not to say, "The greatest productive force is human selfishness" (*LL*, 349). But of course he means that responsible self-interest de Crèvecœur spoke of, anticipating the "invisible hand" economics of Adam Smith in his *Wealth of Nations* (1776). According to Smith, a Scottish Calvinist after all, the individual by pursuing his own interest "frequently promotes that of society more effectually than when he really means to promote it." Guided by the "divine hand" of the "Director of Nature," the capitalist is but clay on the divine potter's wheel. D. D. Harriman, for example, takes no personal credit for the socially useful results of his heroic space enterprise.

God does not reward His own work. Therefore, as no man need commend himself, so also he is not obliged to serve the public welfare out of some uneasy sense of social duty, at bottom a response to envy.

The truly responsible person is responsible first of all to himself. "Duty is a debt you owe to yourself to fulfill obligations you have assumed voluntarily" (LL, 353), as did Heinlein himself in signing up for a military career. The self-respecting person acts alone or cooperates as he chooses by his own lights; he never ventures to promote the public welfare as a defense against the guilt-makers, jealous as ever of assertive individuality, whose leveling appeal is: It's expected of you.

Indeed, Heinlein makes a point of hitting at that false code of social expectations that goes by the name of altruism. For him, altruism is no social ethic to begin with. Lazarus Long explains. "Beware of altruism. It is based on self-deception, the root of all evil" (LL, 248). Against that, "Being generous is inborn; being altruistic is a learned perversity. No resemblance—" (LL, 352). This is the same lesson taught by Heinlein's fellow conservative, the great Dr. Samuel Johnson himself. He says it is personal and not public benevolence that counts in life. No wonder that even he is in disrepute in these days of the welfare state.

But note that for Heinlein generosity is a trait "inborn"; it is not a social ideal that one learns to live up to. Again, this is good Calvinist doctrine. The trait belongs to those who have the right charitable stuff by nature; gallantry is their mark of grace. That is the way they are, elected for a trust they have no motive to abuse by concerning themselves with charity as a petty self-defense against the delusive call to altruism. It is their thing, implanted in a minority of mankind for its own good. It is they, when they enlist themselves for duty and responsibility, who advance the human cause. For it is only they who embody the cosmic purpose in things, leading it on. That some few men are aware of their true calling in this is the point of Lazarus Long's notation, "The two highest achievements of the human mind are the twin concepts of 'loyalty' and 'duty.' Whenever these twin concepts fall into disrepute— get out of there fast!" (LL, 247). When its Great Men are no longer respected for their vocation, that society is doomed; it is too late for the Carlyle-like hero to save it, and he is better rewarded on some new frontier.

Thus Heinlein heroes never choose themselves for the larger purpose they serve. Basic to Calvinistic doctrine, the world is divided between the elect and the nonelect (points 1 and 4 made at the Synod of Dort).

Lazarus Long puts it this way in secular terms: "All men are created unequal" (*LL,* 243). Heaven or Hell, none have a say where they go. The elect can no more earn their state of grace than can the damned undo their predetermined doom (points 2 and 4). Election is particular and selective. Or to repeat what Lazarus Long says, "Natural laws have no pity" (*LL,* 351). As ever in Calvinism, it is impossible to place oneself in the scheme of things by a personal decision (point 3). The saints reveal themselves for what they are, when the time comes to show their stuff, their sinful failings otherwise forgiven. But the damned are fallen in their sinfulness forever (point 5), their fatal flaw of character given them to act out by their own free will as they think it to be.

Chapter Nine
Stories of Damnation
and Salvation

God in his mercy chose to save some few sinful human beings, although justice suggests the damnation of all. Or so runs Mark Twain's logic in "The Damned Human Race." For Heinlein, however, the human species is itself a chosen race among all other forms of intelligent life in the universe. We humans therefore have before us an unlimited evolutionary future, thanks to our few elect whose God-given work is to advance our manifest destiny. Indeed, Lazarus Long himself, in one of his many occupations, had once acted as the "Supreme High Priest of the One God in All His Aspects and Arbiter Below and Above" (*TEL,* viii).

The one exception to this optimistic outlook is "The Year of the Jackpot" (reprinted in *The Menace from Earth*). This unique story offers a telling contrast, pointing up Heinlein's usual play on Calvinist mythology. The story begins with a normal Heinlein hero, marked by some particular mark of grace. In this case he is a statistician, gifted with the uncanny ability to chart the common trending pattern in all sorts of seemingly unrelated events. What he sees coming is a mighty convergence of disasters; this year will be the "year of the jackpot" when everything goes wrong. All but his comradely girl friend think he is crazy, as the couple head for the hills with survival gear. Reaching their mountain hideaway outside Los Angeles, they find refuge there just in time. The city is hit one after the other by earthquakes, tidal waves, and Russian missiles armed with atomic warheads. Safe from all that, the end is not yet. The sun explodes as well, and there will be no saving remnant, no Gideon's band to carry on the life of the species. But this outcome is atypical, showing only that Heinlein can do the ultimate disaster story with the best of them.

Also atypical is "By His Bootstraps" (likewise reprinted in *The Menace from Earth*), Heinlein's one story dealing with individual damnation. First published under the byline of Anson MacDonald, it is not part of the Future History series in which exemplary heroes are the rule.

But in this case, deviation from the rule makes Heinlein's favored story line all the more evident, on the principle of pattern contrast. Any pattern is hard to spot in and of itself, until juxtaposed and contrasted with its opposite. Thus the antihero of damnation points up the irresistibility of grace imparted to the usual heroes of election, insofar as a reprobate shows himself no less able to resist his own assigned fate. Here is displayed the darker side of point 2 of the Synod of Dort.

The antihero of the ironically titled "By His Bootstraps" is one sinful Bob Wilson, reprobated for all eternity because in him selfishness never goes beyond self-interest of the most limited sort. At the start of the story he is writing a Master's thesis and not caring much about it. "Get it done, was his only thought" (*Menace*, 39). And his purpose in doing it is no less lackluster, as he looks ahead to more of the same, "the petty drudgery and stuffy atmosphere of an academic career" (54). The subject of his careless and slipshod thesis is the nature of time and he writes, "Duration is an attribute of consciousness and not of the plenum. It has no *Ding an Sich*" (39). Which is to say, the whole of space filled with matter has no suchness in and of itself; it is an attribute of the individual consciousness, supposedly real but beyond objective knowledge. This is a solipist maxim, quite suited to a man with no sense of vocation; and Bob Wilson's adventures turn out to be a gloss on that vain, self-centered, and intellectually prideful philosophy.

When a Time Gate opens in the wall of his little study, he takes it as a calling to greatness made easy. Stepping through the Gate is another Bob Wilson who leads him through it to meet an elderly man called Diktor (an older version of Bob Wilson himself), whose turn it is to say, "There is a great future in store for you and me, my boy— a great future" (45). What Diktor wants from Wilson is the fetching of Hitler's *Mein Kampf*, Machiavelli's *The Prince*, and Dale Carnegie's famous book on how to influence people, plus recordings of sensuous music, for which little trouble he proposes much. "I am offering you half a world in return for a few hours' co-operation" (61). The world in question lies thirty thousand years in the future. Here is where the other side of the Time Gate is located, in the Hall of the Gate in the High Palace of Norkaal. It's a shadowy world of the lazy man's power fantasy, a kingdom of childlike subjects and Playboy bunnies for idle sport. It looks like something for nothing, and Wilson (in one of his three younger avatars) plays along, thinking himself chosen for some higher destiny beyond his halfhearted academic hopes. But of course, the elect never can elect themselves, and the Time Gate is no more than a projection of Wilson's yearning to escape the empty life of his own limited making. But as he learns, he cannot escape his personal Hell. His attempts to undo the inevitable are in fact the punishing chores of his eternal perdition. "A great future!" is the bitter closing.

The story line is a circular one as Wilson finally senses the futility of his quest, finding himself on a "damned repetitious treadmill" (52). It begins with the first Wilson at his desk, followed by a second calling him to Diktor and then a third double stepping in for a vain try at stopping the original from taking the bait. The story goes round and round, told each time from the viewpoint of a different Wilson. But there is no getting off the treadmill; "enmeshed in inevitability," he finds "it had always been too late" for that (65). And so it goes. Again and again he "played through the scene to its inescapable climax" (64). Yet he insists, "maybe we can break the chain even now" (57). But he can't, and he asks, "How was it that he had been unable to change the course of events?" (67). After all, he tells himself in his pride, "You're a free agent" (52). But he isn't. In no way can he outwit destiny, no matter how hard he tries. The damned are damned for their faulty character, and that's that. They cannot, by change of heart, lift themselves up to salvation by their own bootstraps. In this, Bob Wilson recalls the titular figure of Edgar Allan Poe's "William Wilson," in which a dissolute student faces his moralizing doppelgänger to no effect, except to kill him and doom his own immortal soul.

The usual pattern, however, is a tale of election, and this is nowhere better exemplified in Heinlein's very first story, "Life-Line." Its hero, Dr. Pinero, is a hero of Puritan pragmatism. His mark of irresistible grace is his gift for seeing things as they are, as against the Fallen who ignore the facts of empirical reality for theory—another form of wishful thinking.

Dr. Pinero, a scientist of dubious academic credentials, has invented a "chronovitameter," which is his capital asset in his one-man business, Sands of Time, Inc. Advertising himself as a Bio-Consultant, what his machine does, when his clients are hooked up to it, is to predict with infallible accuracy the date of their death (for proof, it also works backward, registering the date of birth). The only time he ever doubts its capacity is when Lazarus Long comes in for a reading (reported in *Methuselah's Children*).

But the machine clearly works as advertised, and for this reason alone does the insurance industry, dependent on the prior invention of actuarial tables, take Dr. Pinero to court. He is, after all, spoiling the basis of its business. Fearing innovation, the insurance magnates are happy to win the support of the Academy of Science, whose dignified members also have their grievance against Pinero, a mere upstart in their eyes. They claim his invention is impossible because its actual results accord with none of their scientific theories; he is giving science a bad name. So together, the Academy and the leaders of the insurance industry bring Pinero to court on charges of fraud. But the judge exonerates Pinero, and the magnates resort to having him murdered by hired thugs.

After the trial, Pinero is visited by newspaper reporters. They test the machine, verifying its accuracy on birth dates; but they are too cowardly to want to know their death dates, which Pinero then places in sealed envelopes. Following Pinero's murder (known to himself, of course, to the exact moment), they reenter his office and burn every envelope, all except Pinero's, which they open with astonishment. He had what they have not, the capacity to face unpleasant facts. That is his gift of grace, to accept the determination of destiny. It is a quality of character given to this "Miracle Man from Nowhere" (*PTT*, 24), as he is tagged in the press, a perfect sobriquet for one of God's elect. For he did indeed come to the fore out of the nowhere of the world's beginnings, not at all earning his gift but that he accepted it.

All of this is made evident in the very workings of his machine. Explaining it to Rogers, one of the reporters calling upon Pinero during their first visit, Pinero says,

Imagine this space-time event which we call Rogers as a long pink worm, continuous through the years, one end at his mother's womb, the other at the grave. It stretches past us here and the cross-section we see appears as a single discrete body. But that is illusion. There is physical continuity to this pink worm, enduring through the years. As a matter of fact, there is physical continuity in this concept to the entire race, for these pink worms branch off from other pink worms. In this fashion, the race is like a vine whose branches intertwine and send out shoots. Only by taking a cross-section of the vine would we fall into the error of believing that the shootlets were discrete individuals. (*PTT*, 20)

Or as Lazarus Long says, " 'No man is an island—.' Much as we may feel and act as individuals, our race is a single organism, always growing and branching" (*LL*, 245). This notebook entry, interesting to reflect on, starts off with a quotation from John Donne's famed seventeenth-

century sermon, collected in *Devotions* (1624), which came to popular
attention after Hemingway used another phrase from it as the title of
his *For Whom the Bell Tolls.*

What could be more obvious? Pinero's chronovitameter belongs not
to the realm of engineering possibility, but to that of Calvinist mythology.
Its workings reveal a theological truth, cast in the language of Darwinian
biology: we individuals are but organic parts ("pink worms") of a
supra-individual organism that is the species *Homo sapiens.* The actions
of its members are not unrelated to the evolutionary dynamics of the
human race as a whole. Its more assertive types are by nature contributing
parts to the hidden purpose of things, which is the salvation of the
human race; that is, its immortality as a racial being. Men are mortal
(those pink worms), but Man is not. A species of intelligent life that
carries the likes of Dr. Pinero in its collective pool of genetic resources
is all the stronger for it, in contrast with Heinlein's aliens.

They, too, are single organisms (like the Little People, or the Bugs
or like those who judge Kip and Pewee), but their collective unity is
composed of like parts with no inequalities to set off one from another.
None are distinctive individuals, none are of the elect; all are damned
without condition. And although the human species has its intrinsically
bad men, like Bob Wilson, they are but part of its diversity and
strength, vis-à-vis the aliens, who are monsters of amoral collectivism;
they lack selfhood in any respect. Their weakness is a static and stolid
uniformity. But the human thing is dynamic, given its diversity of
organic parts, good men and evil; and the moral struggle between them
is what makes for evolutionary change and progress. Dr. Pinero's example
is revealing in showing the right stuff mankind has to prevail. As
Heinlein says elsewhere, "Life belongs to those who do not fear to lose
it" (*DS*, 109).

Dr. Pinero's most distinctive trait, his courage to face the inevitable,
is the gift of his inborn disposition to respect empirical reality. He
trusts the results of his machine while the Academy scientists do not.
They are comic figures unable to understand anything except through
theory. Their being made objects of comedy for that shows how far
Heinlein goes in drawing upon Calvinist mythology. Nothing more
reveals the lasting Puritan impress on American letters than a recurrent
harping on the tension between pragmatism and urbane learning. Why
else should Heinlein find it a point to score, over and over again, by
taking sides on this nagging issue? In *Number of the Beast,* for example,
he goes out of his way to state what might seem obvious, that "an

observed fact requires no proof. It simply *is,* self-demonstrating. Let philosophers worry about it: they haven't anything better to do" (158). Or as Lazarus Long is moved to say, "If it can't be expressed in figures, it is not science; it is opinion" (*LL,* 240).

This latter surely is overstatement, but it does betray Heinlein's concern with a matter endemic to classical American letters. Mark Twain summed it up when in chapter 43 of *A Connecticut Yankee* (1889) he said, "How empty is theory in the presence of fact!" Before him it was Cooper's obsessive concern, as in *The Prairie* (1827), one of the five "Leatherstocking Tales" that told about Natty Bumppo the frontiersman. In a major scene, going on for several chapters, Natty out on the Western plains meets with a naturalist from the Eastern seaboard, a Dr. Bat who has pompously latinized his name as Dr. Battius. A hot discussion arises between them as to what is the proper name for the animal, the "hump" of which is roasting in Natty Bumppo's campfire. Dr. Bat has trouble accepting the fact that the buffalo, as Natty calls the animal, has a "hump" to begin with because the animal is from the viewpoint of scientific taxonomy not a buffalo but a bison; therefore, the "savory core" of buffalo meat roasting in the fire cannot be as tasty as Natty avers. There being no hump in the meat of the true buffalo, Natty has to be wrong in offering such a morsel for a reason no more sufficient than his misnaming of the animal. And so the dispute arises "between these two men, of whom one was so purely practical and the other so much given to theory" (chap. 7). Natty finally replies, "Why, man, you are further from the truth than you are from the settlements, with all your bookish l'arning and hard words . . . . [T]he piece in your hand is the core of as juicy a buffalo hump as stomach need crave" (chap. 9).

Yet Dr. Bat insists otherwise, saying to Natty, "your system is erroneous, from the premises to the conclusion; and your classification is so faulty, as utterly to confound the distinction of science. The buffalo is not gifted with a hump at all; nor is his flesh savory and wholesome." He is then told, "The man who denies that buffalo meat is good, should scorn to eat it!" Even so, Dr. Bat has to say he sees differently, "Not with the organs of sight; but with the more infallible instruments of vision: the conclusions of reason, and the deductions of scientific premises" (chap. 9).

For Cooper, of course, it is Natty Bumppo's empircism that wins the debate solely because he leads the border life; he is a man "of great simplicity of mind, but of sterling worth. . . . He was a man endowed with the choicest and perhaps the rarest gift of nature, that of distinguishing good from evil." In other words, the hero of practical reality is above all a moral hero. Only this kind of man, as with Heinlein heroes endowed with the same gifted horse sense, is elected to further the human cause. Or as Natty says in his extreme old age to Dr. Bat, after a long life of self-reliant adaptation to frontier conditions, "that I am still here, young man, is the pleasure of the Lord, who has spared me until I have seen fourscore and laborious years, for his own secret ends" (chap. 10). So it comes on a note of irony when Dr. Bat is given the last word, claiming himself to be "one who, I may say without vanity, has some insight into the mysteries of nature" (chap. 12). But his vanity is that of the Academy of Science given to the persecution of Dr. Pinero, in a replay of Galileo's trial, in which the great astronomer was convicted for the evidence of his telescope, that the earth revolved around the sun. "Nevertheless—it *still* moves," he said in words exactly repeated by the hero of Heinlein's "Universe," a story in which a lost starship is not believed to be the self-enclosed moving thing it is among the stars (in *Orphans of the Sky*, 49). The geocentric view of the world dies just as hard as does the egocentric one, which is Bob Wilson's fallacy. How vain is his theory that he is a free agent in the outwitting of destiny—which personal mistake is the very sign marking his damnation.

Heinlein heroes, by contrast, never go against destiny. They are its agents; they are chosen, they respond with no questions asked. Sometimes they are aware of the cosmic process (as Dr. Pinero surely was), and sometimes not, as is the unassuming hero of "Misfit," the second of the Future History stories after "Life-Line."

It is the story of Andrew Jackson Libby, a young boy with a famous Christian name and a common surname. He joins the Cosmic Construction Corps of A. D. 2105. Its initials, the CCC, recall those of the Civilian Conservation Corps of the 1930s during the Depression era; and its purpose is much the same: to give unemployed youth a new start. In this case, the boys in question are assigned to an asteroid with the job of repositioning it by the force of implanted rocket tubes, so that it may serve as a convenient way station for the further exploration of deep space. It is to be officially named E-M3 after it is properly placed.

Andrew Jackson Libby is among a number of boys assigned by the Federation of terrestrial states to E-M3, where they are told by their duty captain about their opportunities for a new start in life. Back on

Earth they had been "misfits," but now, "everyone of you starts even today" (*PTT*, 636). All of them are now situated on the frontiers of outer space, and it remains to be seen who among them will make the most of that challenge. In the event, it is Andy who shows his stuff when the time comes, his hidden mark of grace revealed under stress. His peculiar gift is his "intuitive knowledge of arithmetrical relationships" (649).

The boys are told, "What we have to do is part of a bigger scheme. You, and hundreds of thousands like you, are going out as pioneers to fix up the Solar System so that human beings can make better use of it" (635). But things go wrong from the start, when the ballistic calculator miscalculates the charging of the rocket tubes. Only Libby, with his intuitive gift, spots the error; and he does not fail to make a fuss about it, even though he is gigged for insubordination. Brought before his operational captain, he is proved correct, and the explosive charges are recalculated. "Well done, E-M3" radios the chief of operations from his flagship (643). Thus has Libby's gift contributed in some small way to that "bigger scheme" that is Man's cosmic adventure.

On the other hand, other Heinlein heroes are quite conscious of their calling to serve that "bigger scheme" of things. Delos D. Harriman is the most notable in this regard, and he first makes his appearance in "Requiem," the third of the Future History stories. The title derives from the Requiem Mass for the repose of departed souls. That Harriman dies in repose is clear from the epigraph, taken from a poem by Robert Louis Stevenson, which is inscribed on his own tombstone in Samoa, far from his native home. The poem speaks to that circumstance. Here the poet "lies where he longed to be, / Home is the sailor, home from the sea." It is the same epitaph rudely inscribed over D. D. Harriman's hasty grave on the moon. It "was scrawled on a shipping tag torn from a compressed-air container, and pinned to the ground with a knife (*PTT*, 245). But Harriman, the great opener of mankind's new frontiers, would have been happy enough with that. The why of such a pathetic and makeshift grave for one of Carlyle's Great Men is of course the whole burden of the story. But it is enough to cite the poetic lines in question, which read:

> Under the wide and starry sky
> Dig the grave and let me lie.
> Glad did I live and gladly die,
> And I laid me down with a will.

So it is with Harriman; this is "where he had longed to be—he had followed his need" (261). Here, under the starriest of skies, he laid himself down with a will.

But why here, to die on the moon of old age and of the strains of space travel only minutes after his arrival? For all that, "He was serenely happy in a fashion not given to most men, even in a long lifetime. He felt as if he were every man who has ever lived, looked up at the stars, and longed" (259f.). His particular death, in other words, shares in something universal, belonging as well to those others elected by destiny to serve the same purpose. In following his personal need he did not die alone, but in the spiritual company of all those others obsessed by the Wonderful Dream.

But the full story of Harriman's ambition was told ten years before in "The Man Who Sold the Moon," an original contribution to a collection of Future History tales published under that title in 1950. Thus "Requiem," dealing with the end of his career, was written first. Cooper similarly wrote the story of Natty Bumppo's last years in *The Prairie* (1827), before detailing his beginnings in *The Pathfinder* (1840). In both authors, characters carry over from one story to another, a practice known to world literature from Balzac to Thackeray and Trollope.

But what is uniquely American to Heinlein's treatment of Harriman is the social import of his life and death, as this yields to a Calvinistic reading. The most decisive clue to this line of interpretation comes from one of Heinlein's fantastic stories, almost always paired by the critics with "All you Zombies—" as a solipsist tale. They could not be more mistaken. The story in question is "They" (*Unknown,* April 1941; reprinted in *6 x H*).

The hero of "They" is a nameless individual, speaking for the genius of the human race at its best. He is isolated in a lunatic asylum under the care of the Glaroon, in his human disguise as Dr. Hayward, confined there for treatment of paranoia. The Glaroon, as later revealed in *Job,* is a subcontractor in the business of cosmic architecture under Koshchei. In "They" the Glaroon (or Dr. Hayward) works for "the First for Manipulation," perhaps one of Koshchei's appellations if not of some other power above him in the Great Architect's overall hierarchy. Yet the narrator-hero does indeed seem to be a paranoid case of the wildest sort. He thinks that the material world around him, and all the people in it, exist only for one purpose—to deceive him. The whole purpose of things is to keep him from distinguishing "their" lies from his truth, "to prevent me from realizing that I was at the center of their arrangements" (*6 x H,* 142). In the event, he is right; "they" are indeed no more than "swarms of actors" put into his familiar world to deceive him. "They looked like me, but they were not like me" (140f.).

It would spoil the story to tell how he stumbled onto this truth by recalling a not-so-trivial event that occurred on the outside. But never mind; the main thing is, he must verify this truth on the inside, where he is forced by default to deal with a problem of epistemology in its purest form. Testing a number of theories regarding the origin, nature, methods, and limits of human knowledge, he makes a special point of dealing with solipsism—Bishop Berkeley's theory that only the self exists, or can be proven to exist. In that exercise he too has no other recourse than to fall back on his own being as the only possible starting point. "First fact, himself" (143). But he comes to a different conclusion. Not for him the false logic of solipsism, made fun of in the limerick that goes:

> There was a faith-healer of Deal
> Who said, "Although pain isn't real,
> If I sit on a pin
> And I puncture my skin
> I dislike what I *fancy* I feel![1]

No; when he kicks a stone, Samuel Johnson's refutation of Bishop Berkeley, he knows the pain is real. "He knew that he did not invent the information brought to him by his senses." Or again, "There had to be something out there, some otherness that produced the things his senses recorded" (143). Illogical as this may be, the narrator trusts to his five senses alone, grounding his knowledge of reality in nothing more than his innate horse sense.

Mistrusting theory and logic and everything he had ever read in books, he saves himself from illusion in the ultimate test of self-reliance. That sense of alienation he once felt turns out, he discovers, to be the very object of the big lie focused on him alone, a deception induced in him by way of breaking down his heroic selfhood, at the same time detaching him from any sense of kinship with his fellow human beings. The truth is, now the lie is penetrated, he is the last holdout among his kind, still endowed with that self-assertiveness essential to a free human being, in a world dehumanized in accord with the soulless and collectivist designs of the Glaroon. It is only the narrator's inner light to see things as they are that stands in the way of the Glaroon's complete victory. And so the world is saved by a lone genius of puritanical empiricism against all efforts by Dr. Hayward, under the cover of psychiatric therapy, to talk him out of his faith; nothing in the way of the doctor's pretended fellow feeling, nor any of his logical and theoretical arguments, has any effect.

Sensing the truth at last, the narrator is filled with gladness.

Gladness everywhere! It was good to be with his own kind, to hear the music swelling out of every living thing, as it always had been and always would—good to know that everything was living and aware of him, as he participated in them. It was good to be, good to know the unity of the many and the diversity of the one. (6 x H, 149)

Here the hero makes mystical contact with the racial being of his own species. Not alone after all, he is game to spend the mortality of his individual life in and through the biological life of the human organism, which has its collective immortality assured in the leading qualities of just such cranky individualists. In finding his gladness in that awareness of all humanity, the narrator stands for that relationship between the universal and the particular that makes men what they are. By virtue of their outstanding exemplars, men are able to understand themselves as a part of the species (the universal), while yet retaining their individual selfhood (the particular). It is a human joy to know the unity of the many (all diverse individuals collected within a single organism of racial scope) and the diversity of the one (each contributing to the organic whole in his own personal way).

This dynamic interaction between the one and the many is what gives men their racial strength to endure anything. Hence those alien powers in "They" fail to conquer its hero and make him surrender his will to selfhood to their collective designs. They know only the one in the many, without knowing the many in the one. For them, the collective organism is all, the individual nothing. Their efforts to undo him, mankind's last hope, are doomed to failure. Their plan to remake humanity in their own monstrous image has only this one man's heroism to check it. But all it takes is one Great Man, as Carlyle says, to see through the "sham" of existing institutions. When the time comes, ever and again, the Hero leads the way toward a future of progressive change and renewal in that cosmic theater of events that is human history. The hardiness of the human species owes everything to its exemplary members; they make mankind what it is in its potential for evolutionary growth.

By the end of the story the aliens—or are they gods?—consider packing up their stage sets and going away. Heinlein's aliens are at times as hard to distinguish from gods as gods are from giants in Norse mythology. For all their godlike powers, however, both aliens and giants are no final match for men in their seeming puniness. In one exceptional case, the aliens are quite literally "higher" beings of earth's evolutionary history who live in our stratosphere. Derived from Sir Arthur Conan Doyle's "The Horror of the Heights" (1913, collected in *The Conan Doyle Stories* of 1929), they appear (unseen) in "Goldfish Bowl," which concludes with the greatest punch line in the history of science fiction. The story's hero, "a superior kind of *Homo sapiens*," is caught up by these beings and kept as a pet, as we keep goldfish. His problem is to warn his fellow humans of this hovering presence, which he solves as he nears death by scarifying with a thumbnail the brief yet revealing message on his naked, disposable body. It is picked up in the Pacific Ocean by the U.S.S. *Mahan,* named after Capt. Alfred Thayer Mahan, author of *The Influence of Sea Power on History* (1890), the doctrinal basis of President Theodore Roosevelt's imperial policy. Human imperialism now has its challenge marked out plainly enough in the scar-tissue message, which reads, "BEWARE—CREATION TOOK EIGHT DAYS."

At all events, the efforts of those ambiguous beings in "They" to "dismantle" the human "system" (the dynamic interplay of its individual/collective makeup) run into such difficulty, when faced with the natural aptitude of just one man to see through their shams, that they are prepared to admit defeat. The Glaroon, in the guise of Dr. Hayward, had tried to instruct his patient in a paranoid fantasy, by way of breaking him to a sense of isolation from his own kind—the first step that any regime of despotic socialism tries in atomizing the individual for selfless duty to a collective cause totally devoid of volunteer support. Failing that try, the Glaroon is reduced to one last desperate expedient.

The Glaroon now recommends to the First for Manipulation the ultimate therapy: "Prepare to graft the selected memory track at once." There's nothing for it at last but to alter the patient's consciousness so as to weaken his powers of volition. This order is passed on to the First for Operations (yet another level in the hierarchy of cosmic architects and stage builders), whose reply is, "It would be simpler if we understood his motives." But the Glaroon (closer to the problem, after all) is more cautious. Voicing his doubts to the First for Operations, he says, "but if we understood his motives, we would be part of him. Bear in mind the Treaty!" (152).

What Treaty? It seems to be some artistic principle or guild rule, set by the Great Architect himself, that makes it impossible to tamper with human individuality once the design feature of volition was built into human creatures from the start. Lowly as they are, they exult in one quality lacking in their jealous creators. For the gods to understand what they have created would mean their surrendering whatever powers were left to them to administer after the fact, and these are no more than clerical powers over the hierarchical offices of their own ponderous bureaucracy. The Treaty seems to acknowledge a divine status for humans beyond the reach of their creators to change by administrative fiat. Volition was given them and it cannot be taken back or altered.

The final blow to the Glaroon comes when the actor he assigned to play the patient's wife asks for one small sympathetic favor on his behalf. "You are becoming assimilated!" the Glaroon says (153). Thus to understand humans, itself a humanlike act of empathy, is to assimilate to them. Fearful of losing their godhead, "they" retire from the field of envy. It has, at last, no shaping power.

No zoo-life for humans in the recreational yards of the gods playing at world-building. In that respect, the story is a paradigm of human affairs, gods or aliens notwithstanding, in which the collectivist idea has no force over free men. Insofar as the spirit of self-interest is the natural and spontaneous way of relating the precocious individual to the achievement of the species, no better service can be done it by artificial means. No socialist zoo for man, contrived on a misunderstanding of human nature by the planners of the planned life. Opposed to this is the Calvinist ethic. While its theology is determinist, it yet accommodates free will and spontaneity; men who accept this doctrine are expected to work hard, given whatever gifts of grace it is theirs to receive as a mark of necessity, in their feeling responsible for the deathless progress of the human adventure. Election proceeds from predestination in such a manner that the cause of it is found in the character of the gifted themselves.

That Heinlein takes the problem of the one and the many as the subject of his most philosophical of stories is not incidental. The idea is displayed, ever and again, in the naming of many of his heroes. For example, Andrew Jackson Libby ("Misfit"), Daniel Boone Davis (*The Door into Summer*), Sam Houston Jones ("Logic of Empire"), and of course Woodrow Wilson Smith, also known as Lazarus Long (*Methuselah's Children, Time Enough for Love,* and elsewhere). And this is not to overlook Delos D. Harriman ("Requiem" and "The Man Who Sold the Moon"), taking Harriman to represent the pioneering spirit of America's economic heroes, after his robber-baron namesake.

In these names, the universal and the particular are united. Take Andrew Jackson Libby. The surname Libby is a common one, like Smith or Jones. Indeed, Libby is the surname of America's most famous painter of commoners, Walter Libby, who also did a notable portrait of Walt Whitman,[2] the preeminent poet of the nation's democratic multitudes. In this aspect, Libby is everyman, the American universal, itself glorified and upheld by the life of one particular Great Man, as indicated by his Christian name, Andrew Jackson. Jackson, the seventh president of the United States, won that office for being regarded as the leading representative of the frontier spirit. So does Andrew Jackson Libby exemplify that spirit, as his deeds tell in "Misfit" and also in *Methuselah's Children,* where he figures as the designer of a space drive for the starship *New Frontiers,* in which the Howard Families escape from their cave of persecution. He combines in himself the unity of the many and the diversity of the one. "Libby" is the many, a representative of the American race and its nation of nations, whereas "Andrew Jackson" is emblematic of the diversity of the one. The American nation is composed of diverse individuals, given their liberty under the frontier conditions of the New World, a freedom won and preserved for them by their economic and political heroes alike, an elect responsible for the common good as the elite of the Old World never were.

But if the New World is different, unprecedented in being selected to advance the cosmic destiny of the entire planet, it owes to the founding theology of our Puritan forefathers. No less is the same Calvinist premise imprinted in the secular Calvinism of Cooper, Twain, and Heinlein. Their reworking of the old religion is what gives their works the power of a mythology tried and true.

For another example, take D. D. Harriman (or Dee Dee as he is affectionately known to his associates). In himself he represents the whole (the common Christian name Delos) and the part (the exceptional Harriman surname). He is at once everyman and a Great Man. All Americans are free not only to seek their personal salvation, as does Dee Dee in "Requiem," but the elect among them are free above all to do this in the name of racial salvation. Here in America the parts and the whole, the one and the many, are united in social harmony. There is no one authority to dictate the universal; the parts decide that, as each individual works out the nation's common destiny in asserting his own liberty. This practice of generating the universal out of the many judgments of freely acting agents, is what makes for the success of the American experiment. The public good is arrived at by consensus, where free men are given the choice to share in those human dignities they all prize, which are freedom in morals, democracy in government, and private-profit capitalism in economy. No: this is not the Old World, where, as Henry Adams put it in his autobiography (*The Education of Henry Adams,* 1918), an elite is given to establishing moral and political and economic values among the lesser breeds, as time is told from Greenwich.

The American elect, however, tell time from another clock; and it is everyman's time, told by the ticking of "kosmic" destiny. All the same, American democracy is a tricky proposition. Walt Whitman, an American saint if ever there was one, pondered this in his prose, even as he concealed his doubts in his poetry. There he celebrated the intense individualism of the American spirit, a sense of freedom and independence yet compatible with a sense of union. His favorite word for describing that paradoxical pairing of these two sensibilities was the word "ensemble." It means all the parts of a thing taken together, so that each part is considered only in relation to the whole. So in making his poetry about America's democratic multitudes, he did not mean to celebrate its mass per se. In Whitman's ideal, democracy marries "perfect individualism" with "the idea of the aggregate," that is to say, the ensemble. In that regard does he address the question of "the one and the many." He is, as he says, the chanter of the "Many in One."[3]

The latter phrase is explained by Roger Asselineau as meaning that Whitman, worried about the leveling down tendencies of American democracy, attempted in his poetry the countervailing idea of leveling up. "His program called for the building up of the masses by building up grand individuals."[4] For example, his eulogy of General Grant in *Specimen Days* (entry for 28 September 1879) following his world tour as ex-President: "What a man he is! what a history! what an illustration— his life—of the capacities of that American individuality common to us all."

In this, Whitman took his cue from Emerson ("every great institution in the lengthened shadow of one man") and Carlyle ("history is made by its Great Men"). In taking the "Many in One" as a justification for his praise of the democratic one in the many, he did the right thing. If our nation is to be a model for the rest of the world, even for the rest of the universe, then it is our heroes of the American experience who are destined to show the way.

So it is with Heinlein heroes. Their work may be seen as a gloss on one of Whitman's final poems, written in his extreme old age, "One Song America, before I Go." It is all the more apt to cite here as Heinlein, at this writing, lies gravely ill in his own old age.

> One song, America, before I go,
> I'd sing, o'er the rest, with trumpet sound,
> For thee—the Future.
>
> I'd sow a seed for thee of endless Nationality;
> I'd fashion thy Ensemble, including body and soul;
> I'd show, away ahead, the real Union, and how it
>   may be accomplished.
> (The paths to the House I seek to make,
> But leave to those to come, the House itself.)
>
> Belief I sing—and Preparation;
> As life and Nature are not great with reference to
>   the Present only,
> But greater still from what is to come,
> Out of that formula for Thee I sing.[5]

Chapter Ten
A Comedy of Errors

To end on a lighter note, here is a cautionary, the-joke's-on-me tale that advises the reader to be his own judge in finding the meaning of Robert A. Heinlein. Fiction is by nature ambiguous; and while it may have a message to send, it doesn't come by way of Western Union. The writer of short stories and novels, unlike the essay writer, doesn't tell you what he means, he shows you. He shows his meaning indirectly in a series of piled-up dramatic images, with only a few bits of pointed rhetoric here and there. The basic message is: enjoy the story, relish the storyteller's art, and if you find anything else in it, all well and good.

This is what Heinlein implied in his parting words. "Tell your students it's all entertainment," he said as he saw me to the door. But of course he slyly hinted at something more. . . .

Entertainment, yes. Heinlein writes with a lively and unfailing sense of humor, and that in itself is basic to his appeal. The medium is the message, insofar as the most lasting impression made by his work is the very tone of the author's voice and temper. Even to be in the presence of the man himself is to be invigorated by a youthful and uplifting spirit, the same unbeatable optimism that captures his multitudinous fans as they joyfully take to the most serious of his moral lessons. Like Mark Twain, who called himself a "week-day preacher,"[1] Heinlein knows how to enliven the Sunday pulpit preachings that once passed for entertainment in the collected sermons enjoyed by our more sombre colonial ancestors.

Although impatient with this comparison when I put it to him ("I'm not a Calvinist!" he said, the sunshine dimming), we both had a good laugh over it in the end, when he easily disposed of my critical pretensions regarding "Coventry." As it happens, I had pressed him on this one particular story because my students were no less unhappy with my Calvinistic reading of it. Knowing that I was on my way to visit Heinlein following the spring semester of 1984, they delegated me to raise their doubts at that time. This I agreed to do, promising to report back at a class reunion, which I did—only to reveal that we'd all been wrong on every point, according to the author's own testimony. This is the comedy of errors I conclude with, as a warning to all literary critics. We none of us have the right answers. Henry James was correct: our business is to share our enthusiasm for the author's art, not to explain it.

At all events, "Coventry" is the one story my students have disputed ever since I began teaching the Heinlein course. On other stories, they more or less go along with my line of interpretation, but never on this one. Here, they claim, I force a pattern where it doesn't fit. One of them was honest enough to cite Emerson against me, in words entered into every dictionary of quotations, "A foolish consistency is the hobgoblin of little minds."

For example, everything goes well when I talk about *Starman Jones* (1953), one of Heinlein's best juveniles. Here a young boy seems to work his way up from steward to astrogator. Max Jones begins working in the holds of a passenger starship, cleaning catboxes for pets belonging to the ship's ritzy passengers, one of whom he romances and marries in the end. What happens in between is, the ship gets lost in hyperspace. Grounded on a distant planet, far from any place listed on the star charts, the ship loses its astrogation tables as well. It is young Max who saves the day, bringing the ship back home, after the captain appoints him chief astrogator.

This ought to be the impossible promotion because the astrogator's guild is closed to all but hereditary members. The rules are not unlike those described by Mark Twain for "The Pilot's Monopoly" in chapter 15 of *Life on the Mississippi* (1883), only they are more rigid. The guild is a veritable caste not open to outsiders, whatever their talent. Yet Jones wins his place in it when the captain notices he has all the tables in his head. How can this be allowed, given the astrogator's cast-iron monopoly? Max is a mathematical genius, to be sure, like Andrew Jackson Libby. But Libby is given his chance to show his stuff under freer frontier conditions. What gives Max the opportunity to show his under opposite conditions enforced by guild rules?

It turns out that Max had memorized a library of space manuals belonging to a dead uncle who once had been a guild member in good standing. So Max's talent and saving genius is legitimate after all. He both earns and socially inherits his position of authority in the control room, much to the captain's relief. He has what it takes to begin with, inherently, in addition to his claim to hereditary guild membership.

So far so good when it comes to classroom discourse. The students agree that if Max has the right stuff, it does indeed owe in part to a genetic line differing from that of ordinary folk. (The same with Kip and Pewee, both of whom are children of brilliant and accomplished scientists and mathematicians.) Yet what Max has by advantage of the genetic lottery, he has also by his learned abilities in applying himself to memorizing his uncle's space manuals. Max makes use of his innate potential only because he is disposed to cultivate it, which sorts with his unusual sense of duty and loyalty. This quality, in the end, is what brings the ship and its passengers home safely. When called upon, he was the right man to be chosen, for his character, his inheritance, and no less the studiousness of his work habits.

None of this fails to win the students' agreement, reducing my teaching job to little more than making explicit what they appreciate in Heinlein by intuition. They know they are not geniuses, yet Starman Jones is a boy they can relate to and take as a model in perfectly good faith. (So is Pewee for the girls in *Have Space Suit—Will Travel*.) They, too, are permitted to sense themselves chosen above others for some responsibility attaching to the professional careers ahead of them. Heinlein tells them, in effect, they need not feel guilty about their superior prospects in life, nor feel ashamed of whatever competence they have in their own measure. He assures them they rank among the elect at least for their willingness to hit the books hard in their studies. As Heinlein says (to repeat), "I don't write for stupid people," and it is true in my experience that lackluster students do not take very keenly to him. As for the bright ones (his fans to begin with), he warrants a high-spirited sense of confidence, endorsing their take-charge, can-do, keep-those-caissons-rolling-along attitude. In this, he induces in them the old-time puritanical sense of a "vocational calling."

At the Illinois Institute of Technology, the Ethics Center reflects that religious tradition. Its interest is to uphold the old puritanical idea of job responsibility in the various professions for which we train our graduates, mainly in the engineering sciences, architecture, industrial and product design, city planning, and business management. There is always a bottom line below the bottom line, and that is duty and loyalty to the task—or is it a transcendental line? Whatever, the students who also attend the Heinlein course get a double dose of the same values. But in truth, they prefer to get their Sunday ethics from a favorite author who in his weekday preachings rather shows than tells them what he means.

Yet when it comes to my theological reading of "Coventry," the students invariably balk. The title means a place of exile, named after a city figuring in the English Civil War between Puritans and Royalists, and it is one of the Future History stories. It takes place in the postrevolutionary society of the Covenant, this term referring to a social contract drawn up after the overthrow of the Prophet's theocracy in " 'If This Goes On—.' " Of course, this has biblical overtones, derived from the Old Testament agreement between God and the ancient Israelites, in which God promised to protect them if they kept His law and were faithful to Him. It also figures in the ecclesiastical language of the Calvinist church, as a solemn agreement between its members to act together in harmony with the precepts of the gospel.

But in the Heinlein story, it is "the first scientific social document ever drawn by man." Citizens are "forbidden by the Covenant to damage another," something that "can be pointed to and measured," unlike the prescientific concept of "justice" (*PTT,* 622f.). The students are quick to point out, however, that "damage" can mean anything, and so is no more scientific than any other social concept. But I persuade them to pass over this point, allowing the author his pragmatic convention, in light of his puritanical mistrust of theoretical abstractions. They have only to be reminded, in getting around this matter, of Lazarus Long's notebook saying, "If it can't be expressed in figures, it is not science; it is opinion" (*LL,* 240).

The story's hero (or so I used to name him) is David MacKinnon, who violates the Covenant by taking a poke at someone who swore at him (insulting words don't count as damage, as do sticks and stones and punches to the nose). MacKinnon is then tested by psychometricians, who find him unsocial by nature. The sentencing judge, who reports on these tests to the offender, tells him that they "show you believe yourself capable of judging morally your fellow citizens and feel justified in personally correcting and punishing their lapses. . . . From a social standpoint, your delusion makes you as mad as the March Hare. . . . To Coventry with you" (*PTT,* 588).

Coventry lies beyond a "stasis barrier" that cannot be crossed except under the controls of a gatekeeper on the outside, and on the inside all Covenant-breaking reprobates are trapped. MacKinnon had the choice of accepting psychological rehabilitation, when "sentenced to choose between the Two Alternatives" (*PTT,* 585). But he chooses Coventry, thinking that there he will find a "Crusoe-like independence." He passes through the gate in his armored vehicle, a "steel tortoise," capable of defending a solitary life come what may on the other side. But the narrator comments on this romantic delusion: "It did not occur to him his chattel was the end product of the cumulative effort and intelligent co-operation of hundreds and thousands of men, living and dead." Human culture and its technology is a product of history and man's ongoing functional interdependence (the point made before in "The Roads Must Roll"). But "that did not prevent him from believing that his native intelligence and the aid of a few reference books would be all that he would really need to duplicate the tortoise, if necessary" (590).

Once on the other side of the barrier, in Coventry, he finds not the land of anarchic freedom he expected, but a world of thuggery and competing Mafia-type groups. Shortly after his arrival, as it happens, they finally bury their differences and work together for the purpose of breaking out and attacking the United States with a newly discovered weapon. Like the hero of Edward Everett Hale's "The Man without a Country" (1868), MacKinnon had said on being sentenced, "I hope I never hear of the United States again!" (587). But his patriotism is excited when he learns of this revolutionary plot from Fader Magee, who turns out to be head of the Secret Service. (*Fader* is Danish for father.)

Magee escapes in some mysterious way not described, to warn of the revolution brewing inside. MacKinnon follows, not knowing that Magee had preceded him. MacKinnon gets out by swimming under the barrier where it crosses a river, in a miraculous escape described as such. MacKinnon rejoins Fader Magee, learns for the first time who he really is, and then signs up under him for work in the Secret Service. This he is able to do easily enough because the rules of the Two Alternatives are waived for him. After a brief interview with the psychometricians who had first diagnosed him to be a sociopath, he is permitted to reenter the world of the Covenant without undergoing rehabilitation, as is required for all who decide to come back. Thus is MacKinnon revealed to be one of the elect, never sick to begin with; thereafter he comes to work as Fader Magee's right-hand man.

To this conclusion my students object. How can that be? Was MacKinnon not diagnosed as being sick by the psychometricians of a scientific society? A number of rebuttal papers were prepared and duplicated for circulation in class. The best one, the students agreed, suggested that MacKinnon had been reborn, and that swim under the barrier was the moment of his election—he got grace by conversion.

But I replied that rebirth is inconsistent with Calvinist doctrine; one is elected at birth, or not at all. Given the irresistibility of grace (point 2 in the Synod of Dort), it is no more possible for the damned to lift themselves to grace by their own bootstraps (the case of Bob Wilson) than it is for the elect to resist being saved. One need not lead a blameless life to be chosen for one's predetermined election for the doing of good works. Or again, point 5 speaks to the perseverance of the saints, and has it that election is founded not upon foreseen faith but upon God's good pleasure. The sainthood of the elect is revealed for what it is, when even the worst sinner is given his assigned good work to do, and it is preserved thereafter.

For example, there is the blind poet of the spaceways in "The Green Hills of Earth." He was a terrible rogue and a writer of dirty doggerel verse to boot, before he was blinded by an accident on board a great spaceliner in which he served as jetman. The ship's automatic system for shutting down its reactor motor when overheated didn't work and so he, without a moment's thought, shuts it down with the manual controls, losing his eyesight to the intense radiation in the very heart of the engine room. When duty called, he did not hesitate as did the other jetmen. No longer able to work at his profession, he thereafter bummed around the Solar System, composing a new and finer kind of verse about the planets and the spaceways as he remembered them in his youth. Nearing old age, he cadges a ride back home to the green hills of earth (not so green anymore), when a similar accident happens. Knowing his way by touch in the engine room, he kills himself reaching into the atomic reactor with a pair of tongs in his naked hands to fish out the exploding fuel. Appropriately, he is not remembered for this selfless deed, but for his finest poem, composed while he worked and picked up by mikes in the engine room and recorded in the captain's cabin. It is "The Green Hills of Earth," full of nostalgia for old Terra before it was abandoned by the pioneers of outer space. The sainthood of the deed, but one heroic act among all the others that helped to further man's cosmic density in his conquest of space, is forgotten. Yet all of them are given their apotheosis in his remembered poetry, celebrating the thundering jets that carry the sons of Terra outward to those new frontiers where mankind is finding its renewable future. Good works belong not to the person but to the purpose in things.

Unconvinced by this example, the students always insist that the Synod of Dort does not apply to "Coventry." MacKinnon, they argue, showed himself to be a romantic if not a rugged individualist, for which the psychometricians of the Covenant rightly diagnosed his illness. No way around that. No way to say he was not sick to begin with. Either that swim under the barrier is a symbolic conversion (disallowance of that by the Synod of Dort not withstanding), or else he is no saint after all.

Such is the puzzle I was urged to lay before Heinlein. He had two surprising answers, which I duly reported back, with enough deflating embarrassment to go all around.

As for the question of MacKinnon's being diagnosed sick by the psychometricians, "they made a mistake," Heinlein said. So much in support of points 2 and 5, it would seem. MacKinnon had the right patriotic stuff in him all along, despite his asocial attitude earlier on. Even his worst sin, his hatred of the United States, is redeemable because it was he in the end who was a chosen instrument for saving it from a gang of evil-minded revolutionaries. What a blow this was to the students and their critique of the story, made all the heavier because Heinlein's answer devalued their faith in his talk about a scientific society, always of much appeal to engineering majors; they easily are led on to dreams of social engineering. But supposing, horrible thought, all this enlightened rationalism, as with the Covenant society, has its limits? Perhaps Heinlein is more subtle than any of us guessed, in having some reservations about that puritanical pragmatism I myself was overready to stress. If "they made a mistake," then Lazarus Long's remark on the merits of science over opinion is to be taken with a grain of salt. The human element is impossible to delimit in any social code; social control is beyond the reach of any covenant devised in the name of political science.

But the final blow fell on my head most especially, when Heinlein revealed that I was wrong in naming the hero of the story. MacKinnon is not the hero, he said; "he's just a chorus to Fader Magee." He who sitteth at the right hand of the Father in Heaven belongs to another and altogether subordinate realm, as perhaps do all so-called Heinlein heroes. Perhaps all of them are likewise impersonal agents of the Cosmic Purpose. As Lazarus Long says, "racial survival is the *only* universal morality" (*LL,* 242f.).

In the end, Heinlein is closer to Emerson than he is to Carlyle when it comes to the role of the hero in history. In *Representative Men* (1850), Emerson says, perhaps responding to Carlyle's idea of the Great Man in *Heroes and Hero-Worship,* that humanity is not the mere sum of its individuals, whatever his emphasis on self-culture. Humanity is rather one cosmic unit suffused with the spirit of the Deity; so that a great man is but one who represents more of this divine essence than his fellows. He thus shows mankind as a whole how to appreciate its own possibilities.

Chapter Eleven
Last-Minute News

As this book goes to press, there is late news to insert here under a final chapter heading. The Admiral has returned to work with enough vigor to perfect the typescript of opus 189 (hereafter *MJ*), and he looks to seeing it issued on his eightieth birthday, as expected before his recent illness. It is not possible at this time to say what title the publisher will settle on, but the author's is, *"To Sail Beyond the Sunset"* (a phrase from Tennyson's *Ulysses*). Subtitle is, "The Life and Loves of Maureen Johnson (Being the Memoirs of a Somewhat Irregular Lady)." Citations are from a MS copy received at the very moment this book was readied for production.

Maureen Johnson Smith (b. 4 July 1882) is the mother of Lazarus Long (b. Woodrow Wilson Smith on 11 November 1912). In the end, she is translated by a space-time shifter, the Gay Deceiver (see *Number of the Beast*), from Tellus Prime in 1982 to Tellus Tertius (a third Earth), there to be rejuvenated and to marry her son in Galactic year 4324. It turns out that Lazarus Long (returned from the future as Captain Ted Bronson) did not perish after all on the battlefields of World War I, following the passionate love affair he had with his mother on the night of 29 June 1918 (the year is 1916 in *Time Enough for Love*), when Woodrow Wilson Smith himself was but a small boy. (Time paradoxes don't bother Heinlein one bit.)

But more, Maureen also marries her father, Ira Johnson, M.D. (b. 1852), whose removal to the future is the basis of the novel's plot, a task carried out on her behalf by the Circle of Ouroboros and its Time Corps, of which Lazarus Long is a leading member. These examples of incest, however, have no tragic overtones as in classical literature.

They rather form part of a utopian world of "omnigamous" unions imagined by Charles Fourier in his *Le Nouveau monde amoureux* (The New World of Love), published for the first time in English in 1971.[1] The Howard Families, following "The Great Diaspora of the Human Race" (*TEL,* ix), is at last united in one big omnigamic family, a Society of Love, whose members are by now all of them descendants and collaterals of Lazarus Long; with "Human" standing as a figure of speech (the part equals the whole) for the totality of Lazarus Long's cosmic progeny. Added to them, finally, are his mother and her father, the genetic source of Lazarus Long's unique and saving hereditary variation. The pioneering of D. D. Harriman's new frontiers is accomplished to completion by this one man; the new Earth is his lengthened shadow.

In "A Message to the Berkley Sales Force concerning *The Cat Who Walks through Walls*,"[2] Heinlein touches on *MJ*, his next work. "I've always wanted to have a book banned in Boston; *Maureen Johnson, An Irregular Autobiography*, should be banned in Las Vegas" (*ST*, 8). But not even a rejuvenated Henry Miller could manage that these days.

And while Heinlein claims opus 189 to be "totally lacking in any redeeming social value," it is evident that he thinks otherwise; especially when he smugly predicts that *MJ* will not be found "ideologically correct by the standards of the literary establishment" (*ST*, 7). He may rightly expect that, given his carefree allusions to "Dr. Fraud" and the "malevolent silliness of Marxism" (*MJ*, 255, 551). Psychotic fads such as these, led by "Revisionist intellectuals," have lost Americans "the hard common sense that had won them a continent. By the sixties everyone talked about his 'rights' and no one spoke of his duties—and patriotism was a subject for jokes" (*MJ*, 102, 552).

Clearly, Heinlein is once again as facetious as Mark Twain in claiming no moral value for his work. Indeed, Sam Clemens gets more than a dozen references and at least one appearance in *MJ*, and for good reason. Maureen's father is a friend and correspondent, and a framed letter from Twain hangs in his surgery in Butler, Missouri. He is just as much the crusty aphorist as is Lazarus Long, not surprising since both characters seem to resonate with the kind of influence Heinlein says his grandfather Alva E. Lyle (another country doctor like Dr. Johnson) had on himself. Maureen is no less her father's protégée, even learning chess from him at the age of four, as did Heinlein from Dr. Lyle. Nor is the author's love of cats overlooked (Pixel figures again as in *Cat*). Maureen says, "How you behave towards cats here below determines your status in Heaven" (*MJ*, 244). The point seems to be that cats are emblematic of unsullied human dignity, as displayed in their pristine good manners.

Be that as it may, it is likely that Heinlein critics (as he predicts) will find *MJ* " 'self-indulgent' " (*ST*, 7). It is not that. To say so is to dismiss the serious antirepressive theory behind the novel's clinical talk about sex (as Maureen learned it from her father Dr. Johnson) and its shameless exercise. Inasmuch as Heinlein writes as a public educator, and always has, in this case it appears that he is addressing a new generation of sex-educated youths. Perhaps only he can get away with persuading them to take "orders" of seeming irrelevance from their parents, whom he backs up when it comes to forbidding promiscuity and drug taking as well in favor of homework, if the kids are to learn how to cope with the even more arbitrary ways of the outer world.

Indeed, Heinlein is all the more topical in having Maureen face the problem as a divorced, single parent, when he has her speak of a weaker sister in the same situation:

I despise most in Marian her self-indulgent failure to carry out the parental duty of maintaining discipline. "Spare the rod and spoil the child" is not sadistic; it is hard common sense. You fail your children worse if you do not punish them when they need it. The lessons you fail to teach them will be taught later and much more harshly by a cruel world, the real world where no excuses are accepted, the world of TANSTAAFL and of Mrs. BeDoneByAsYouDid. (MJ, 584f.).

There is also much more on male duties, in this time when so many men shrug off their responsibility to pregnant women and young children. Maureen says, "A male must be willing to live or die for his female and their cubs . . . else he is nothing" (573). For all of Lazarus Long's other faults, he never abandoned wife and child.

But there is a larger lesson MJ attempts to teach. The usual language of sexuality in the modern novel either exalts Eros in a triumphant climax (the sacred approach) or it diminishes Eros in some climactic anguish (the sex-hating demonic approach). Heinlein occupies the middle ground between these two extremes, giving sexuality a sustained note of continuous interest, and that always neutral, neither apologetic nor vindictive in tone; the effect wanted is that of unspoiled innocence.

This is dangerous ground, never before held with success. Indeed, Italo Calvino wonders if there is any place at all in literature "for the debunking purpose of a direct, objective, dispassionate representation of sexual relations as facts of life amid all the other facts of life. If this attitude were possible, it would not only occupy a central position, opposed as much to the internal censorship of repression and hypocrisy as to sacred or demonic speculations on Eros, but it would without the least doubt be the victor, clearing the field of all opposition. The literary experience of the last fifty years, however, convinces us that this position remains an intellectual and would-be enlightened pretension."[3] The real question for the critics to address, then, is whether or not Heinlein is the first novelist to prove Calvino's judgment premature.

At all events, Heinlein's daring gambit may at least draw attention to his usual line of culture criticism, now stated as a general concern for the "decline and fall of the United States" as part of "The Twentieth Century Devolution" (*MJ*, 543, 549). Things have come to a pretty pass, but maybe his intelligent readers can help hold off the evil days for a while yet, as ever doing their spiritual father's (or Dutch uncle's) chivalric work in a foreign country. Among the particular evils he itemizes are too many lawyers (Maureen had studied law only to protect herself from them), family decay, high taxes, decline in rational thinking, entertainers and high-paid athletes mistaken for important leaders of public opinion, strikes by public officials, peer-group promotion in public schools, declining literacy, and, last but not least, dirty rest rooms (a sign of declining courtesy and polite concern for others). All these things, Maureen observes before she departs for Tellus Tertius, "have destroyed the best culture up to that time in all known histories" (551).

Even so, she has the secret of salvation, given her on the night of 29 June 1918, when her son came to her in the person of Captain Bronson, with his pillow talk about things to come. This she then reveals to D. D. Harriman, knowing now the success of his Moonship, offering him also the monies she has invested in the Howard Foundation, a big sum, thanks to her lover's tips on the stock market. This is the same Foundation that, under Lazarus Long's later chairmanship, pays the way for the Howard Families' Great Diaspora.

Meeting D. D. Harriman with this outcome in mind, Maureen looks into eyes that "burned with fanatic fervor—he made me think of those Old Testament Prophets." Dee Dee replies, now that Harriman Industries are bankrupt and the old man's Wonderful Dream is in sheriff's trouble, "It's good to know you have faith in us." Maureen: "It's not just faith; I'm certain." She knows his ship will fly, and many others afterward, in the name of free enterprise. "You are manifest destiny, Sir! You will found Luna City . . . Freeport for the Solar System!" (536).

Could anything be more determinist? Heinlein himself speaks to the power of Calvinist mythology when he has Maureen say, there is no paradox between free will and "the golden chains of predestination." "Free will is a fact, while you are living it. And predestination is a fact, when you look at any sequence from the outside" (463). This recalls what Bob Wilson in "By His Bootstraps" has to say about creating the same hellish scene of his perdition over and over again by his own free will. Human will is " 'free' to the ego, mechanistic from the outside" (*Menance*, 83). From God's point of view (or from the cosmic outlook of space-time mechanics), "causation can be completely circular" (58).

Sadly, though, Tellus Prime is doomed. So it is on each of the six time lines monitored by the Circle of Ouroboros. Each one goes its different way from about 1939, the year Heinlein began writing his Future History series, followed by other kinds of stories and their alternate worlds. All are code named by the Time Corps after the first man to land on the moon, Leslie LeCroix in number two (Maureen's time line and Harriman's), Neil Armstrong in number three (our time line) and again in the sixth one (and there are all the others hinted at in *The Number of the Beast*). Yet all six of them and their stories are part of the one story Heinlein has to tell. He never felt obliged, at the urging of John Campbell, his early editor, to stick with his Future History format. From the start the author had his own vision of artistic unity, no matter what; every contrasting line of storytelling builds toward a "making strange" effect on our own lives and times.

Above all, in every time line it's goodbye to Tellus Prime, "Man's Old Home," "mankind's beautiful bride." "I remember Earth," says Maureen, "clean and green" (*MJ*, 257). Beyond the sunset—is that, to recur to the novel's title, where now lies man's "Only Home"? (540). The answer rests with the title's allusion to a line from Tennyson's *Ulysses*, yet another reworking of Homer's *Odyssey*. And as the original odyssey (the very byword for a journey) is the story of a return, it might well be asked, what is this Only Home to which mankind returns?

"To Sail Beyond the Sunset—." It is an evocative title, recalling the ideal heroic spirit Tennyson had in mind in recreating his own version of *Ulysses* (or Odyssus, if you prefer Greek to Latin). James Joyce, while composing his, came up with the defining phrase: "Ulysses, the wanderer, the most human, the most complete of heroes—husband, father, son, lover, farmer, soldier, pacifist, politician, inventor and adventurer."[4]

Surely these are the attributes of Lazarus Long as well, he who founded Tellus Tertius, mankind's new bride, populated by the Howard Families; and now, his own bride, among others, is his progenitive mother. This whole world is one happy omnigamic family, a Society of Love for mutual caring and the caring for children, made possible by one man (a new Adam?). The density of kinship relations detailed in *MJ*, complete with a table of the Howard Families, given like a Catalog of Ships in the backmatter and headed "People in This Memoir," is another clue. Lazarus Long's untroubled sexuality seems to be the hallmark of this last frontier, man's Only Home, the innocent home of the original elect of God. Sharing it in a circular way with all of his cosmic seed and those who seeded him, he is the returner of humanity to Eden. The past through tomorrow, indeed! Or in Milton's first lines to *Paradise Lost* (a work inspiring the mock-epic *Lines from the Beginning* in "Universe"),

> Of man's first disobedience, and the fruit
> Of that forbidden tree whose mortal taste
> Brought death into the World, and all our woe,
> With loss of Eden, till one greater Man
> Restore us, and regain the blissful seat. . . .

MJ seems to mark the conclusive end to the whole cycle of Heinlein's work, now that it appears he will write no more. Although his life is not yet over, when the end does come he no doubt is prepared to lay himself down with a will, not unlike D. D. Harriman in "Requiem." A hint of that is foretold in the portrait of the elderly, cane-holding Harriman on the cover of *The Past through Tomorrow*. Here Dee Dee is painted in the very likeness of the Admiral, looking skyward with a wistful yet confident expression that Harriman had on his face when left behind; packed and uniformed for the blast-off, he is not to voyage in the Moonship he dreamed of and built. This new Moses had seen the future, as from a cosmic mountaintop, without being able to join the starters in their exodus to this promised land of his Wonderful Dream.

The dream remains, however, a longing in the hearts of Heinlein fans—make no mistake about it. One of these, a young mathematical genius designing weapons for the Strategic Defense Initiative (SDI, or "Star Wars") at the Lawrence Livermore National Laboratory, also works at designing spaceships powered by atomic fusion. If his fusion ships are to fly, he says, the United States must buy time with SDI. "To me," he says, "working for the future has two parts. One, coming up with spaceship designs to actualize the vision. Two, making sure that the Soviets don't stop us before we're able to get into space in a

big way. After that, I don't care about the Soviets." Speaking like Dee
Dee Harriman he goes on, "I want the future to be up in space because
there is just so much more out there. Here you can't play games with
new political systems because every piece of land is already owned by
someone. It's a zero sum game. Out there, it's absolutely limitless.
Space is one big frontier."⁵ What deeper hopes lie in the imagination
of this young Star Warrior? Inspired by Heinlein, not even the author
of *MJ* himself can say. Nor will the future carriers of the Wonderful
Dream know until they've carried it out, not until it's "Up Ship!"
from Tellus Prime for the last time.

Appendix
The Names of the Beast in *The Number of the Beast*

While most readers seem to have spotted the thinly disguised fact that all of the names of the one Beast are anagrams of my name or one of my pen names, no reader appears to have spotted all of them. I expected the first appearance of the Beast (p. 19 USA, p. 9 UK) to be spotted at once, thereafter the reader would be alert for anagrams in odd-appearing names. Oh, well. Mea culpa.

The first number is the page number in the USA editions; the second number (in parentheses) refers to the UK editions.

19 (9) Neil O'Heret Brian = Robert A. Heinlein

93 (93) Bennie Hibol = Bob Heinlein

176 (177) Morinosky = Simon York (pen name: DETECTIVE STORY, et al.)

262 (273) Iver Hird-Jones = John Riverside (pen name: UN-KNOWN, et al.)

499 (539) The Villains Nine Rig Ruin = Lt. Virginia Heinlein USNR

499 (540) Torne, Hernia, Lien, & Snob = Robert Anson Heinlein

509 (553) Sir Tenderloinn the Brutal = Lt. Robert A. Heinlein USN RTD

509 (554) L. Ron O'Leemy = Lyle Monroe (pen name for SF 1939–46)

510 (555) Mellrooney = Lyle Monroe (pen name for SF 1939–46)

The Beast reveals himself again in the very last line of the table of contents, which then refers to p. 508 (553)—then leaves tracks gross enough for Oregon Bigfoot on pp. 481–82 (518–200).

The nature of this story, fantasy comedy or farce, is emphatically stated in the first line of chapter 1 and this is confirmed in the first four lines of the second chapter. These were intended to prepare the readers for an adventure story in which no one ever gets killed or even hurt, no blood is shed, the White Hats always win, the dead rise up and are restored to the living, and real live franchised citizens of these

United States and of Canada mix freely with fictional characters of many universes.

The cash customers accepted this; I have never before had a book that received such uniformly favorable fan mail. But, with a few pleasant exceptions, the lit'rary critics did not. Nor did any critic spot any of the anagrams or pick up any of the clues.

One would expect even a critic to spot the blatant giveaway in the first fourteen lines of p. 508 (eighteen lines of 552). There is one last major clue, the last line of the book. Yes, *deus volent,* the Beast will be back.

$(6^6)^6 \neq (6)^{6^6}$ Larry Niven pointed this out to me before the story was written; several readers have noted it. This I made explicit as to which expression I meant in dialog on p. 59 (55) and on p. 403 (432)—but on p. 59 the expression had to be ambivalent—no parentheses—in order to wind up with "666; The Number of the Beast."

(Signed) R. A. "Beast" Heinlein

Notes and References

Preface

1. See H. Bruce Franklin, ed., *Future Perfect: American Science Fiction of the Nineteenth Century* (New York: Oxford University Press, 1968).
2. Roger Asselineau, *The Transcendentalist Constant in American Literature* (New York: New York University Press, 1980).
3. Henry James, *Literary Criticism* (New York: The Library of America, 1984), 1:98.

Chapter One

1. This opening gambit is borrowed (and improved on, I hope) from Damon Knight's introduction to Robert A. Heinlein, *The Past through Tomorrow* (New York: Putnam, 1967). Heinlein's Annapolis address of 5 April 1973 was published as a guest editorial in the January issue of *Analog Science Fiction/Science Fact* (formerly *Astounding Science-Fiction*). A tape recording of it titled "Forrestal Lecture at the U.S. Naval Academy" is available from American Audio Prose Library (Columbia, Mo.), order no. 190.
2. See *Expanded Universe*, 447–451, 452f. for his comments on it; hereafter cited in text and notes as *EU*.
3. James, *Literary Criticism*, 1:1236.
4. Cited by Justin Kaplan, *Mark Twain and His World* (New York: Crescent Books, 1982), 174.
5. These examples (and the "high voltage" phrase of Bradbury's following on) are borrowed from Jack Williamson, *People Machines* (New York: Ace Books, 1971), 135f. and 123.
6. Cited by Justin Kaplan, *Born to Trouble: One Hundred Years of Huckleberry Finn* (Washington, D.C.: Library of Congress, 1985), 13.
7. Cited in ibid., 23.
8. *Stranger in a Strange Land* (New York: Avon Books, 1962), 310; hereafter cited in text and notes as *SSL*.
9. *Job: A Comedy of Justice* (New York: Ballantine Books, 1984), 439; hereafter cited in text and notes as *Job*.
10. *Time Enough for Love: The Lives of Lazarus Long* (New York: Berkley Books, 1974), xi; hereafter cited in text and notes as *TEL*.
11. From "The Man Who Sold the Moon," in *The Past through Tomorrow* (New York: Berkley Books, 1975), 185; hereafter cited in text and notes as *PTT*.

12. Damon Knight, *In Search of Wonder: Essays on Modern Science Fiction*, 2d ed. (Chicago: Advent Publishers, 1967). See chap. 7, "One Sane Man: Robert A. Heinlein," 76–89.

13. *The Cat Who Walks through Walls* (New York: Putnam's, 1985), 233; hereafter cited in text and notes as *Cat*. Quotations are from the original hardcover edition.

14. W. D. Howells cited in Benjamin J. Spencer, *The Quest for Nationality: An American Literary Campaign* (Syracuse, N.Y.: Syracuse University Press, 1957), 326.

15. In *School Library Association of California Bulletin*, November 1952. See variorum in *EU*, 373–77.

16. *Podkayne of Mars* (New York: Berkley Books, 1975), 9; hereafter cited in text and notes as *PM*.

17. R. H. Stacy, *Defamiliarization in Language and Literature* (Syracuse, N.Y.: Syracuse University Press, 1977), 2.

18. Bertrand Russell, *Has Man a Future?* (Harmondsworth, England: Penguin Books, 1961), 7.

19. The major serial publication of the Niagara University project is titled *Space Journal*, first issued in 1983. On the L-5 Society, see Jack D. Kirwan, "Mr. Heinlein's Children," *National Review*, 4 February 1983, 122f.

Chapter Two

1. *Double Star* (New York: Signet Books, 1970), 101f.; hereafter cited in text and notes as *DS*.

2. See L. Sprague de Camp, "The Space Suit," *Astounding Science-Fiction* (March 1948), 108–19; this magazine hereafter cited as *ASF*.

3. For two accounts of their trip to the Soviet Union her notes helped to prepare, see " 'Pravda' " Means 'Truth' " and "Inside Intourist" (*EU*, 403–45).

4. *The Rolling Stones* (New York: Ballantine Books, 1952), 53f.; hereafter cited in text and notes as *RS*.

5. Used with the permission of William Drish, who concludes his letter: "I could go on, but the point is this: Robert Heinlein has had a greater influence on my intellectual development than any other author. Now that I am an engineer, I'd like to say, 'Thanks for your help, Mr. Heinlein!' "

Chapter Three

1. William F. Buckley, Jr., *Up from Liberalism*, 25th anniversary edition (New York: Stein & Day, 1984), 182.

2. Marcus Cunliffe, *The Literature of the United States* (Harmondsworth, England: Penguin Books, 1961), 24, n.1.

3. Cited in Gay Wilson Allen, *Waldo Emerson* (New York: Penguin Books, 1981), 422.

4. See Alexei Panshin, *Heinlein in Dimension* (Chicago: Advent Publishers, 1968), 162.

Chapter Four

1. James, *Literary Criticism,* 1:55.

2. In Lloyd Arthur Eshback, ed., *Of Worlds Beyond: The Science of Science Fiction Writing* (Chicago: Advent Publishers, 1947), 11–19.

3. *The Scientific Romances of H. G. Wells* (London: Gollancz, 1933), viii.

4. I thank the Lovecraft fans among my students for recalling this allusion. It is documented in Curtis C. Smith, ed., *Twentieth-Century Science-Fiction Writers,* 1st ed. (New York: St. Martin's Press, 1981), 347. Heinlein, however, says he never heard of Lovecraft's Jonathan Hoag, claiming that he gave much thought to inventing this name on his own.

5. Walt Whitman, *Complete Poetry and Collected Prose* (New York: Library of America, 1982), 1001. The quotation is from the 1872 Preface to *Leaves of Grass.*

Chapter Five

1. Heinlein cited in *10:56:20PM, EDT, 7/20/69: The historic conquest of the moon as reported to the American people by CBS over the CBS Television Network* (Columbia Broadcasting System, 1970), 107.

2. Ibid. Not all that passed between Heinlein and Walter Cronkite is recorded in this book. According to one witness, part of the outtake goes as follows:

HEINLEIN: About one third of the weight of this Apollo ship could have been saved by having an all-female crew.

CRONKITE: Women in space! Never!

HEINLEIN: Eventually whole families will go into space. But in this particular instance, if we'd sent someone—say Peggy Fleming—on this mission, the entire project could save a great deal of money. Because women weigh less than men, and the engineering on the Saturn rocket would have been simpler and cheaper. An athlete like Peggy Fleming could have learned all the things she needed to know, and done what was necessary.

At this point, Cronkite continued to sputter at the idea of women in space as Heinlein again and again tried to reiterate it. The camera crew, who had never seen anyone flap Cronkite before, then applauded. What makes this exchange interesting is that it dramatically reverses all the usual clichés about these two men. While the media critics dub Cronkite the great "liberal" commentator of the TV airwaves, critics of Heinlein attack him for being illiberal, sexist, and antifeminist.

3. See Kenneth von Gunden and Steward H. Stock, *Twenty All-Time Science Fiction Films* (New York: Arlington House, 1982), 14–25.

4. Videotapes of the Tom Corbett series are available from The Nostalgia Merchant, A Division of Media Home Entertainment, Inc. See Fall 1985 Catalogue (Culver City, Calif.), 33.

5. J. O. Baily, *Pilgrims through Space and Time* (New York: Argus Books, 1947).

6. *Fascism,* of course, is a term coined by Mussolini. After sixteen years of abusive use of this term among Heinlein foes, one SFRA critic dared to conclude that it did not, after all, strictly apply to his political thought. See Dennis E. Showalter, "Heinlein's *Starship Troopers:* An Exercise in Rehabilitation," in *Extrapolation* 16:2 (May 1975). 113–24. But this "rehabilitation" saves Heinlein only from the particulars of Italian Fascismo. Thus it is advised that a more honest term of abuse be applied, something more general like "authoritarianism."

7. James Burnham, *Suicide of the West* (Chicago: Regnery Books, 1985), 239f.

8. Both Emerson and Twain cited by Roger Asselineau, "A Transcendentalist Poet Named Huckleberry Finn," in *Studies in American Fiction* 13:2 (Autumn 1985), 223.

9. Whitman, *Complete Poetry and Prose,* 930.

10. Hugh Henry Brakenridge, *Modern Chivalry,* ed. by Claude M. Newlin (New York: American Book Company, 1937), 20.

11. Whitman, *Complete Poetry and Prose,* 1260.

12. John T. McNeill, *The History and Character of Calvinism* (New York: Oxford University Press, 1954), 224f.

Chapter Six

1. Nelson Manfred Blake, *Novelists' America: Fiction as History, 1910–1940* (Syracuse, N.Y.: Syracuse University Press, 1969), 4.

2. See Tony Goodstone, ed., *The Pulps: Fifty Years of American Pop Culture* (New York: Bonanza Books, 1970).

3. Considering that the final title was the publisher's and not the author's, the agonizing by critics over the ins and outs of its philosophical meaning is agony misspent. See especially Robert G. Pielke, "Grokking the

Stranger," in Nicolas D. Smith, ed., *Philosophers Look at Science Fiction* (Chicago: Nelson-Hall, 1982), 153–63.

4. Percival Lowell, *Mars* (Boston: Houghton, Mifflin, 1896), revised in 1909 as *Mars the Abode of Life.*

5. See Luc Sante, "The Temple of Boredom: Science fiction, no future," *Harper's* (October 1985), p. 69. This is the article reprinted in SFRA's newsletter for December 1985. It is a general attack on SF, rebutted by a staff critic (November issue) on every point save its ugly smear job on Heinlein.

6. See unsigned article, "A Martian Model," in *Time* (19 January 1970), p. 44f.

7. Cited in Kaplan, *Mark Twain*, 196.

8. From a Twain speech of 1886, "The New Destiny," cited by Philip S. Foner, *Mark Twain: Social Critic* (New York: International Publishers, 1958), 170.

9. *Robert Heinlein's Starship Troopers: Man vs. Monster: Intersteller Warfare in The Twenty-Second Century,* Bookcase Game no. 820 (Baltimore: The Avalon Game Company, 1976).

10. Twain cited in Kaplan, *Mark Twain*, 58n.

11. William James on Whitman, cited in Justin Kaplan, *Walt Whitman: A Life* (New York: Bantam Books, 1980), 56.

12. *New York Times,* 5 July 1986, p. 7.

13. *New York Times,* 8 July 1986, p. 9.

14. Quoted in the Sunday *New York Times,* 6 July 1986, sec. 4, p. 14, with the headline "Soviet Writers Seek Peaceful Co-Existence with the State."

15. *Fantasy Review,* no. 32 (June 1986), p. 4.

Chapter Seven

1. See Patrick Parrinder, *Science Fiction: Its Criticism and Teaching* (London: Methuen, 1980), 89f.

2. See the squib headed "Contact" in "The Talk of the Town," *New Yorker,* 1 July 1974, p. 17f.

3. Emerson cited in Allen, *Waldo Emerson,* 163.

4. Vincent McHugh, *Caleb Catlum's America* (Harrisburg: Stackpole Sons, 1936).

5. Emerson cited in Allen, *Waldo Emerson,* 364.

6. See Leon Stover, "George R. Stewart," in Curtis C. Smith, ed., *Twentieth-Century Science-Fiction Writers,* 519f.

7. From *Russian-English Dictionary,* 4th ed. (Moscow: State Publishing House, 1959), 315.

8. See also *PTT*, 503, 527, 534, 536, and 565; *SSL*, 285.

Chapter Eight

1. See Eloise M. Behnken, *Thomas Carlyle: "Calvinist without the Theology"* (Columbia: University of Missouri Press, 1978).
2. McNeill, *Calvinism*, 265; Alan Richardson, ed., *A Dictionary of Christian Theology* (Philadelphia: Westminster Press, 1969), 99.
3. Max Weber, *The Protestant Ethic and the Spirit of Capitalism*, trans. Talcott Parsons (New York: Scribner's, 1930); Helmut Schoeck, *Envy: A Theory of Social Behavior*, trans. by Michael Glenny and Betty Ross (New York: Harcourt, Brace & World, 1966).
4. See E. L. Jones, *The European Miracle: Environments, Economics and Geopolitics of Europe and Asia* (Cambridge: Cambridge University Press, 1981). Entering into this work are some of my own thoughts on the envy problem in the Third World (see bibliographic note on my two books on China, p. 248).
5. *Have Space Suit—Will Travel* (New York: Ballantine Books, 1958), 175f.; hereafter cited in text and notes as *HSS*.

Chapter Nine

1. Anonymous limerick in David McCord, ed., *The Pocket Book of Humorous Verse* (New York: Pocket Books, 1946), 220.
2. On Walter Libby, see Paul Sweg, *Walt Whitman: The Making of a Poet* (New York: Basic Books, 1984), 123.
3. Walt Whitman cited in Kaplan, *Whitman: A Life*, 300, 158, 251.
4. In a letter to the author, 15 July 1986.
5. Walt Whitman, *Leaves of Grass* (New York: The Heritage Reprints, n.d.), p. 507.

Chapter Ten

1. See epigraph to Foner, *Mark Twain*, 1.

Chapter Eleven

1. In Jonathan Beecher and Richard Bienvenu, eds., *The Utopian Vision of Charles Fourier* (Boston: Beacon Press, 1971).
2. A tape recording made 26 April 1986, hereafter *ST* (for "sales tape") and quoted from a nine-page transcript. It is indexed as opus 188, together with *Cat*.
3. Italo Calvino, *The Uses of Literature*, trans. by Patrick Creagh and William Weaver (New York: Harcourt Brace Jovanovich, 1986), 67.

4. The James Joyce of Tom Stoppard's play, *Travesties* (London: Faber & Faber, 1975), 62.

5. The math prodigy Rod Hyde cited in William J. Broad, *Star Warriors* (New York: Simon and Schuster, 1985), 130, 140. For Dr. Hyde's reference to Heinlein, see 131. Both are members of the L-5 Society.

Selected Bibliography

PRIMARY SOURCES

Following is a listing of Heinlein's book titles arranged by three categories, all fiction. Nonfiction is passed over, yet some of this is accounted for in *Expanded Universe* (*EU* in text), together with running commentaries that amount to a brief set of memoirs (New York: Ace Books, 1980). This unique collection of fact and fiction must be the starting point for any student of Heinlein's life and work.

Almost all titles listed are the available paperback editions, dated from the first impression, and the place of publication is always New York. The date in brackets is that of the original hardcover edition.

1. Story Collections

Under each title is an alphabetized table of contents, with magazine sources (together with pen names) indicated for the first listing of each story. (Not all stories by the author are represented here.) Abbreviations used: *ASF* = *Astounding Science-Fiction* (later *Analog Science-Fiction/Science Fact*; *F&SF* = *Fantasy and Science Fiction*; *GSF* = *Galaxy Science Fiction*; *SEP* = *Saturday Evening Post*; *SSS* = *Super Science Stories*; *UW* = *Unknown Worlds*.

Assignment in Eternity [1953], Signet Books, 1970.

"Elsewhere" ("Elsewhen") by Caleb Saunders. *ASF*, September 1941.

"Gulf." *ASF*, November, December 1949.

"Jerry Is a Man" ("Jerry Was a Man"). *Thrilling Wonder Stories,* October 1947.

"Lost Legion" ("Lost Legacy") by Lyle Monroe. *SSS*, November 1941.

The Green Hills of Earth [1951], Signet Books, 1951.

"The Black Pits of Luna." *SEP*, 10 January 1948.

"Delilah and the Space-Rigger." *Blue Book*, December 1949.

"Gentlemen, Be Seated!" *Argosy*, May 1948.

"It's Great to Be Back!" *SEP*, 26 July 1947.

"Logic of Empire." *ASF*, March 1941.

"The Long Watch." *American Legion Magazine*, December 1949.

"Ordeal in Space." *Town & Country*, May 1948.

"Space Jockey." *SEP*, 26 April 1947.

" 'We Also Walk Dogs' " by Anson MacDonald. *ASF*, July 1941.

The Man Who Sold the Moon [1950], Signet Books, 1973.

"Blowups Happen." *ASF*, September 1940.
"Let There Be Light" by Lyle Monroe. *SSS*, May 1940.
"Life-Line." *ASF*, August 1939.
"The Man Who Sold the Moon." Original.
"Requiem." *ASF*, January 1940.
"The Roads Must Roll." *ASF*, June 1940.
The Menace from Earth [1959], Signet Books, 1970. (*Menace* in text.)
    "By His Bootstraps" by Anson MacDonald. *ASF*, October 1941.
    "Columbus Was a Dope" by Lyle Monroe. *Startling Stories*, May 1947.
    "Goldfish Bowl" by Anson MacDonald. *ASF*, March 1942.
    "The Menace from Earth." *F&SF*, August 1957.
    "Project Nightmare." *Amazing Stories*, April 1953.
    "Sky Lift." *Imagination*, November 1953.
    "Water is for Washing." *Argosy*, November 1947.
    "The Year of the Jackpot." *GSF*, March 1952.
Orphans of the Sky [1964], Signet Books, 1965.
    "Common Sense." *ASF*, October 1941.
    "Universe." *ASF*, May 1941.
The Past through Tomorrow [1967], Berkley Books, 1975. (*PTT* in text.)
    "The Black Pits of Luna"; "Blowups Happen."
    "Coventry." *ASF*, July 1940.
    "Delilah and the Space-Rigger"; "Gentlemen, Be Seated!"; "The Green Hills of Earth."
    " 'If This Goes On—.' " *ASF*, February, March 1940.
    "It's Great To Be Back!"; "Life-Line"; "Logic of Empire"; "The Long Watch"; "The Man Who Sold the Moon"; "The Menace from Earth."
    "Methuselah's Children." *ASF*, July, August, September 1941.
    "Misfit." *ASF*, November 1939.
    "Ordeal in Space"; "Requiem"; "Searchlight"; "Space Jockey"; " '—We Also Walk Dogs.' "
Revolt in 2100 [1953], Signet Books, 1970.
    "Coventry"; " 'If This Goes On—' "; "Misfit."
6 x H [1959], Pyramid Books, 1961.
    "All You Zombies—." *F&SF*, March 1959.
    " '—And He Built a Crooked House—.' " *ASF*, February 1941.
    "The Man Who Traveled in Elephants" ("The Elephant Circuit"). *Saturn*, October 1957.
    "Our Fair City." *Weird Tales*, January 1949.
    "They." *UW*, April 1941.
    "The Unpleasant Profession of Jonathan Hoag" by John Riverside. *UW*, October 1942.
Three Times Infinity, edited by Leon Margulies. Gold Medal Books, 1958.
    Contains "Destination Moon." *Short Story Magazine*, September 1950.

Tomorrow the Stars, edited and with an introduction by Robert A. Heinlein [1952], Berkley Books, 1967.

Waldo: Genius in Orbit [1950], Avon Books, 1950.

"Magic, Inc." ("The Devil Makes the Law"). *UW*, September 1940.

"Waldo" by Anson MacDonald. *ASF*, August 1942.

The Worlds of Robert A. Heinlein, Ace Books, 1966.

"Blowups Happen"; "Free Men" (original); "Life-Line."

"Searchlight." *Scientific American*, August 1962; *Fortune*, September 1962; and elsewhere.

"Solution Unsatisfactory" by Anson MacDonald. *ASF*, May 1941.

2. Novels

Where in a few cases only one date occurs without brackets, the original hardcover text was consulted. Those titles first serialized are followed by the magazine source.

Beyond This Horizon [1942], Signet Books, 1960. By Anson MacDonald, *ASF*, April, May 1942.

The Cat Who Walks through Walls: A Comedy of Manners. Putnam's, 1985. (*Cat* in text.)

The Day after Tomorrow [1949], Signet Books, 1949. Original title "Sixth Column," by Anson MacDonald, *ASF*, January, February, March 1941.

The Door into Summer [1956], Signet Books, 1975. *F&SF*, October, November, December 1956.

Double Star [1957], Signet Books, 1970. *ASF*, February, March, April 1956. (*DS* in text.)

Farnham's Freehold [1964], Signet Books, 1965. *If*, July, August 1964.

Friday. Holt, Rinehart & Winston, 1982.

Glory Road [1963], Berkley Books, 1970. *F&SF*, July, August, September 1963.

I Will Fear No Evil. Putnam's, 1970. *GSF*, July, August, October, December 1970.

Job: A Comedy of Justice [1984], Ballantine Books, 1984.

Methuselah's Children [1958], Signet Books, 1960. *ASF*, July, August, September 1941.

The Moon is a Harsh Mistress [1966], Berkley Books, 1968. *If*, December 1965; January, February, March, April 1966.

The Number of the Beast, Fawcett Columbine, 1980.

Podkayne of Mars [1963], Berkley Books, 1975. *If*, November 1962; January, March 1963. (*PM* in text.)

The Puppet Masters [1951], Signet Books, 1951. *GSF*, September, October, November 1951.

Starship Troopers [1960], Signet Books, 1961. *F&SF*, October, November 1959.

Stranger in a Strange Land [1961], Avon Books, 1962. (*SSL* in text.)

Time Enough for Love: The Lives of Lazarus Long [1973], Berkley Books, 1974. (*TEL* in text.) Its two Intermissions, "The Notebooks of Lazarus Long," in *ASF*, June 1973. (*LL* in text.)

"To Sail beyond the Sunset—." MS dated 1986. (*MJ* in text.)

[Note added in press: Some of the above titles with Signet Books are now being reset for Baen Books (dist. by Simon & Schuster). They are the story collections *Assignment in Eternity, The Green Hills of Earth, The Man Who Sold the Moon, The Menace from Earth,* and *Revolt in 2100;* and the novels *Methuselah's Children* and *The Day after Tomorrow.*]

3. Juveniles

The dates indicate hardcover publication by Scribner's; magazine sources for prior serialization are not given. Citations are from the collected edition reprinted in paperback by Ballantine Books, as Del Rey SF Adventures, between 1975 and 1978, with many impressions thereafter. Two titles belonging here, *Starship Troopers* and *Podkayne of Mars,* are listed with the adult novels above because their original concept as juveniles is not advertised. *Between Planets* (1951); *Citizen of the Galaxy* (1975); *Farmer in the Sky* (1950); *Have Space Suit—Will Travel* (1958, *HSS* in text); *Red Planet* (1949); *Rocket Ship Galileo* (1947); *The Rolling Stones* (1952, *RS* in text); *Space Cadet* (1948); *Starman Jones* (1953); *Tunnel in the Sky* (1955); *The Star Beast* (1954); *Time for the Stars* (1956).

SECONDARY SOURCES

This is a brief selection, limited to illustrating the negativism of the SFRA academics and the divided views of the SFWA writers.

Aldiss, Brian W. *Billion Year Spree: The True History of Science Fiction.* Garden City, N.Y.: Doubleday, 1973, 228f., 269–74. Britain's outstanding science-fiction author here serves up Heinlein with a tone of mockery approaching contempt.

Franklin, H. Bruce. *Robert A. Heinlein: America as Science Fiction.* New York: Oxford University Press, 1980. Belongs to the academic canon of Marxist literature, in its use of Heinlein as a vehicle for hostile culture criticism.

Olander, Joseph D., and **Martin H. Greenberg,** eds. *Robert A. Heinlein.* New York: Taplinger, 1977. Contains nine topical essays by various academics, treating of oedipal conflicts, social Darwinism and the like. The one positive essay is by Jack Williamson, both teacher and writer, on the juveniles.

Panshin, Alexei. *Heinlein in Dimension.* Chicago: Advent, 1968. The first
    book-length study of Heinlein's work, done by a writer credited with
    a Nebula Award. Its loaded biographical approach has much influenced
    the style of later academic criticism.

————and **Cory Panshin,** *Science Fiction in Dimension.* Chicago: Advent,
    1976. Contains a chapter, "Reading Heinlein Subjectively," which
    extends the approach of the above title.

Robinson, Spider. "Robert A. Heinlein: A Sermon." In *Destinies* 2:3. New
    York: Ace Books, 1980. The subtitle of this sermon by a fellow writer
    tells it all. It is, "Rah, Rah, R.A.H.!"

Slusser, George Edgar. *The Classic Years of Robert A. Heinlein.* San
    Bernardino, Calif.: Borgo Press, 1977. Pursues the same Calvinistic
    mythology traced in my own work on H. G. Wells, but with mixed
    feelings about its constraints on the art of story telling.

————. *Stranger in His Own Land.* San Bernardino, Calif.: Borgo Press,
    1976. Argues that the later Heinlein fails his early promise. Professor
    Slusser won the Pilgrim Award for 1986 from the SFRA.

Index

120320